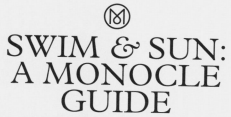

SWIM & SUN: A MONOCLE GUIDE

Hot beach clubs | Perfect pools | Lake havens
PLUS: a big splash of sunny après-swim living

First published in the United Kingdom in 2023
by MONOCLE and Thames & Hudson Ltd,
181a High Holborn, London, WC1V 7QX
thamesandhudson.com

First published in the United States of America
in 2023 by MONOCLE and Thames & Hudson Inc,
500 Fifth Avenue, New York, New York, 10110
thamesandhudsonusa.com

MONOCLE is a trading name of Winkontent Limited

© 2023 Winkontent Limited of Midori House,
1 Dorset Street, London, W1U 4EG

British Library Cataloguing-in-Publication Data
A catalogue record for this book is available from
The British Library

Library of Congress Cataloging-in-Publication data
available upon request.

For more information, please visit *monocle.com*

Designed by MONOCLE
Proofreading by MONOCLE
Typeset in Plantin

Printed in Italy by Rotolito
ISBN 978-0-500-97857-3

Cover image
Havnebadet in Aarhus by Daniel Gebhart de Koekkoel

SWIM & SUN: A MONOCLE GUIDE

Hot beach clubs | Perfect pools | Lake havens
PLUS: a big splash of sunny après-swim living

Contents

Introduction

Whether you like the water to be nerve-tingling cold or Mediterranean warm, the restorative, life-affirming power of going for a swim is undeniable. As you head out to the island in the bay, or aim for the floating dock in the lake, you can be all alone yet supported by the water and, in seconds, something magical happens – the mind clears, the muscles stretch, the pressures from a day of work dissolve. It's easy to see why swimming becomes addictive, how it becomes such an essential part of people's daily routines. And, what's more, unlike many sports and exercise regimes, swimming is not something just for the young. Indeed, the understanding of the value of taking your time, and of finding your own pace, that comes with age makes swimming a pursuit at which many an octogenarian thrives.

When we decided to make a book about swimming we wanted to embrace this watery, health-giving, democratic world but we also wanted to celebrate the rituals, the life, the après-swim pleasures that are attached to this activity. Bodies drying off on the deck of a lakeside bathing club in the heat of summer, kids backflipping with glee into deep mountain lakes, riversides where picnics and wine are consumed after a dip in the current. And we also wanted to celebrate the very architecture and design of the places where we love to swim, from Hungarian bathing venues to Italian beach clubs.

Swim & Sun: A Monocle Guide is a book that knows where to find a remote beach where you can go for a skinny dip unobserved, but which also revels in the pleasures of an urban splash. The revival of many lidos and swimming complexes has been an important addition to many cities – and, again, because they are places not just for perfecting your butterfly stroke but for being with friends, taking time out. Thankfully these are not places to be checking messages on your phone.

MONOCLE, not just this book, has been shaped by swimming – the lure of water. Visitors to our Zürich headquarters are often entreated to walk the short distance to Badi Utoquai (*see page 230*), one of the many bathing clubs on the city's lake, for at least a plunge (and hopefully, in summer, a glass of rosé from the kiosk). And don't think you can dodge the dive by saying you have forgotten your swimwear because someone in the office will no doubt offer a spare. Team reporting trips to Lebanon have taken in Beirut's numerous beach clubs – in Budapest too. Quite a few editorial projects have been hatched under sun-faded pool umbrellas, feet still in the water. Many editorial conferences, reader events, have somehow ended up involving a refreshing, levelling swim at the end of the day.

So while this book does not come in a waterproof plastic zip-lock bag, we hope it does more than look good on your coffee table. As with everything we do at MONOCLE, we want this book to deliver inspiration, encouragement and guidance. As you dive into the pages, we hope you will see places you'd like to one day visit, ventures to emulate in the city where you perhaps live, and people – young and old – who know that an afternoon at the pool, a swim in the lake, a float in the salty ocean is just what they need to make their day. These are the places we've visited and loved. Come on, let's swim – it will do us the power of good.

Andrew Tuck
Editor in chief, MONOCLE

I.
On the coast

There's something exhilarating about swimming in the ocean – the sand that seems to follow you for weeks and the tanned, salty skin that lingers (but never long enough). But it's also about everything else: the long trek to a deserted stretch, the colourful towels expertly placed on a crowded beach and *fritto misto* served with a view. And, of course, that first cocktail as the sun begins its own dip below the horizon. In this chapter we celebrate swimming on – or perhaps off – the coast, from bountiful beach clubs and ocean baths to spectacular hotel pools in seaside resorts. Dive in, no doubt you'll emerge salt-crusted and sunkissed.

Bondi Icebergs Club
Australia

The extraordinary setting and turquoise waters of the rockpool at Sydney's Bondi Icebergs swimming club make it instantaneously recognisable in Australia and beyond. Perched on the edge of the Pacific Ocean, at the south end of Bondi Beach, this landmark club dates back to 1929 and gets its name from the blocks of ice that are thrown into the main pool every May to mark the beginning of the winter season. Both of the pools (there's a shallow one for children) are open to the public for a fee – adult day passes are AU$8 (€5) – but if you aspire to join this most elite of Sydneyside clubs you'll have to prove your swimming chops: the historic Rule 15B states that members must attend three out of four Sundays every month for five years (and those who don't need a good excuse). Once you're a member, you'll be known as an "Iceberg". The club has a sauna on the pool deck level and the dining room and bar are guided by chef Alex Prichard. Make sure to book a table in advance and order a *sgroppino* (lemon sorbet with prosecco and vodka) to finish a meal of fresh seafood or wagyu tagliata.

Go with the flow: Australians are serious swimmers. Be warned that anyone who chats or lingers in the fast lane will get swiftly moved on.

Big splash: Every year the Bondi Icebergs Club fills with spectators for Water Polo by the Sea, a four-day international water-polo event.

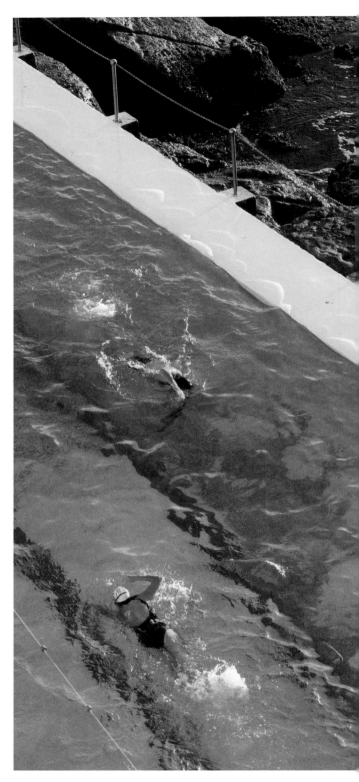

Mezzatorre Hotel & Thermal Spa
Italy

On a craggy promontory overlooking the Tyrrhenian Sea is a terracotta-toned 16th-century watchtower, home to the impeccable Mezzatorre Hotel & Thermal Spa. The building is set on the northern tip of Ischia, the largest of Italy's Phlegraean Islands, and boasts an unrivalled seaside spot. A horseshoe-shaped terrace is home to the hotel's pièce de résistance: a saltwater pool surrounded by fluttering parasols and towel-clad sunloungers with views of the Gulf of Naples – as well as a set of glamorous guests, who drift from pool to lounger and back again. Stone steps descend into the rocky bay below where you'll find the hotel's private beach club. Plunge into the clear waters from the stone platform and swim among the quietly bobbing boats. Once you're done, hop out and dry off in the sun with time for an aperitivo (or two).

Soak it up: The onsite spa takes advantage of Ischia's natural thermal waters with whirlpool tubs, a sauna and steam room.

Get around: The best way to explore the island is by boat or on one of the micro taxis adapted from Apes, the iconic Italian three-wheeler vans. Perfect for zipping across the hilly, pine-forested island.

Pajol Bar Pecine
Croatia

Pajol Bar Pecine is tucked beside a cliff in the seaside town of Rijeka, its shady thatched awnings enticing those in the know. The crystal-clear waters of the Adriatic glitter invitingly as sunsets put on spectacular shows. But with your back to the bar, the view could hardly be more different: the cranes of the Viktor Lenac shipyard tower over vessels under repair. This is Rijeka's unique charm. Croatia's third city retains some of its traditional industry – and non-conformist attitude – even as the tourism and culture sectors take a greater hold. Pajol Bar mixes the best of old and new: it was among the first of Rijeka's beach bars when it opened in 2011 and remains a refuge today. There's often live music and the owner staunchly refuses to install wi-fi, so visitors have no choice but to ignore their emails and dive into the shimmering sea.

When to go: Pajol Bar opens May to early October, 08.00 until 02.00. That suits everyone from pensioners enjoying their morning constitutional to a younger crowd who come for Friday and Saturday evening concerts.

Dress down: This is not a yacht club with designer labels – come as you are. You'll be mingling with Rijeka's alternative and arty crowd, as well as locals from the Pecine neighbourhood.

Mind the gusts: It's best to avoid swimming when the strong *bura* winds are blowing (mostly between October and April).

Piscina Natural
Simão Dias
Portugal

You have to navigate a steep
and long path before you catch
the first glimpse of this natural
pool on the northern coast of
the slim island of São Jorge in
the Azores. Those who don their
trainers won't be disappointed
– the emerald-green waters
at the end are worth the trek.
Swimming in this spot isn't
really about ease of access,
anyway: an island in the middle
of the Atlantic with no direct
flights to the mainland, São
Jorge is a place for those who
enjoy delving a little further and
discovering somewhere a little
wilder. Lowering yourself down
a step ladder into the bracing
waters makes for an invigorating,
life-affirming kind of swim – one
that halts the breath for just a few
seconds. After a couple of brisk
strokes, perching on the dark
volcanic rocks to rest for a while
in the sun will soothe you with
the kind of humming heat that
reaches all the way to the bone.

Pool hopping: Natural pools dot
the Azores islands. These relatively
calmer bathing spots are sheltered
from the open ocean by a line of
rocks, providing a safe way to brave
the choppy waves.

Sculpted swim: The Samão Dias
is found in Fajã do Ouvidor. It is
one of many *lavas fajas* (lava-created
valleys) on São Jorge and, we think,
the most beautiful.

Xuma Village
Turkey

With its vineyards, rolling hills and sandy beaches, Turkey's west coast could be mistaken for California. And, like the Golden State, it is also home to numerous beach clubs. Xuma Village – perched at the end of the Bodrum peninsula in the once-quiet fishing village of Yalikavak – is one of the best. It's a barefoot sort of place surrounded by verdant gardens and time doesn't seem like an issue either. Tuesdays could be Sundays; Thursdays, Saturdays. But the real selling point is the water: the Aegean feels warmer here, more docile (thanks in part to the calming effect of the sun-bleached hills that frame the landscape). Walk down to the pier and leap into the glistening water – if only to reward yourself with an afternoon spent dozing in the shade.

Beach scene: There's an abundance of beach clubs on Turkey's west coast but not all were created equal – 7800 Çesme and Maçakizi are our favourites in the area.

Plate with a view: You won't need to travel far in search of food – the restaurant at Xuma uses fresh, local ingredients and offers its diners sweeping ocean vistas.

Afternoon delight: Make like the locals and enjoy a cup of *çay* (Turkish tea) with a refreshing slice of watermelon. Try it before moving onto something stronger at happy hour.

Charco de la Laja
Spain

When Tenerife emerged out of
the ocean, the island's volcano,
El Teide, forged a coastline that
would reflect its dramatic origins
in its obsidian cliffs. Atlantic
waves then carved a saltwater
swimming hole into the cool
lava, now known as Charco
de la Laja. Here, a vertiginous
descent down a long set of
volcanic stone steps delivers
swimmers to a natural pool
nestled between the precipice
and the open water. Once
you're in, dip below the surface
to discover a vibrant display
of marine life, nourished and
replenished by the waves
that roll over the edge of the
pool's outermost rocks. But
it's not only the colourful sea
creatures that put on a show:
local teenagers head to Charco
de la Laja in the summer months,
where they scale the craggy edges
and leap acrobatically into the
pool's inky depths.

Before you go: Nature dictates
when you can swim in Charco de la
Laja. Online webcams positioned in
towns on the north coast – including
Puerto de la Cruz, Santa Úrsula and
Garachico – are helpful in determining
how big the swells are on any given day.

Getting there: A drive through
the lush banana plantations of San
Juan de la Rambla is the best way to
access the pool. It's possible to park
on the residential streets above the
Charco, although this can get tricky
during high season.

Barreirinha Beach Complex
Portugal

Smack bang in the middle of Funchal, Madeira's capital city, is the cliffside Barreirinha Beach Complex where bathers of all types congregate to enjoy the sun and water in equal measure. To join them, take the lift or stairs all the way down to the waterfront, framed by a rocky backdrop. The complex comprises a series of tiered concrete sunbathing platforms that descend to the ocean, with ample space to roll out your towel and dish out the customary Portuguese picnic. Barreirinha has been a community hub since the 1940s, popular among locals especially during the hot summer months. As well as the concrete decks, there's a sliver of pebbly beach where bathers can swim out from to reach the floating platform. The entrance fee includes access to sunloungers and changing rooms, as well as the priceless experience of diving into the seemingly boundless azure water.

Sunny sip: Head back up and take a seat at Barreirinha Bar Café across the road. Order a refreshing *poncha* (lemon juice, honey and the local spirit, *aguardente*), served with side of North Atlantic views.

Get lost: Post-swimming, the Rua de Santa Maria is a short jaunt from the complex where you can find shops, galleries and cafés.

Eat in style: Next to the bathing platform is Forte de São Tiago, built in the 17th century to protect the coast from pirates. Inside you can now find Restaurante do Forte.

Athens Riviera
Greece

Many beach-goers treat Athens as a stopover before jumping on a ferry to one of the whitewashed-house islands dotting the Aegean Sea – but they're missing out. The Athens Riviera, as the coastal areas of the city are known, has many swimming spots that feel far from the hustle and bustle, including the golden sands of Kavouri and Astir beaches, and the quieter, pebbly shores of Kladiou Bay. Further from the coast, the natural saltwater Vouliagmeni Lake boasts crystal-clear water served by both sea and thermal springs – and which maintains a pleasant 22C year-round.

Hemmed in by mountains to its east and west, the Greek capital stretches across a basin in the Attica Peninsula, where the sea laps at its southern and northeastern sides. Residents are spoilt for choice. In summer, trams and buses departing from the centre are packed with schoolchildren and workers. A growing "après-swim" culture has also emerged, with scores of cafés, taverns and clubs sprouting along the shoreline, offering fish *mezedes* (the Greek answer to tapas), café frappes and late-night kicks.

Perfect ending: To catch a glorious Greek sunset, head down the coast to the Temple of Poseidon in Cape Sounion, a stunning peninsula at the southern tip of Attica.

Bogey Hole
Australia

This rugged ocean pool on the outskirts of Newcastle, a small city in New South Wales, was hewn from sandstone cliffs by convicts in the early 19th century. Now, at roughly 20-metres long (the pool was expanded to keep up with its growing popularity), it's one of Newcastle's key places for a quick dip away from the town's busy main beaches. Its timeworn chain-link fence gives a utilitarian appearance but it's the only place you'll want to be on a summer's day. Note that the Bogey Hole's temperament is bound to the tide: when it's high, rough surf crashes into the pool, while at low tide it feels serene.

The best time for a swim is at dawn, when you'll be treated to a spectacular Australian sunrise.

Heritage pool: The Bogey Hole is said to be the earliest known ocean bath in Australia and is listed on the New South Wales heritage register. As the story goes, the Commandant of Newcastle, Major James Morisset, demanded it be created for his personal use in 1819.

Getting there: Any ocean swimmer worth their sea salt should try the Bathers Way, a stunning walk along Newcastle's best coastal swim spots.

Note the name: The pool's name Bogey comes from the Aboriginal word meaning "to bathe".

New addition: A metal staircase was fitted in 2016 for better access and increased safety on the slippery rocks.

Praia da Comporta
Portugal

Just over an hour south of Lisbon, the once-lonely fishing village of Comporta is now much-loved by artists, A-listers and surfers, and has been a summer destination for the Portuguese capital's wealthiest families since the 1950s. Although it's no longer the deserted spot it once was, Comporta's seemingly endless stretch of unbroken beach has more than enough space for its fans. With 60km of sandy coastline to play on, swimmers can dip into the refreshing Atlantic waters, while surfers and watersports enthusiasts take advantage of Portugal's unrivalled waves. For those who like their beaches well serviced, Comporta does not disappoint. Look for the thatched parasols and beach bars delivering cocktails and snacks (often straight to your sunlounger).

Fresh from the sea: You'll find some of the region's best restaurants here – head to Sal or Sublime Comporta Beach Club for a seafood lunch on the sand.

Hoofing it: Comporta is known for coastal horseback riding, where riders gallop along the beach as waves crash under-hoof.

Plage de Maora
France

Corsica is a haven of unspoilt
beaches and rough jagged
shores. Other Mediterranean
coastlines may offer beach
clubs and rows of shaded
sunloungers but Corsica retains
some of its undomesticated
wilderness. Plage de Maora
is a long sandy stretch on the
fringes of Bonifacio – a town
on the southern tip of the
French island – which is home
to a rare Corsican beach club.
Maora Beach, as the outpost
is known, can be identified by
its terracotta-toned loungers
and tables in the water (which
provide a refreshing lunchtime
setting). The informal beach club
is the perfect spot to sip rosé
and fruit-festooned cocktails
post-dip while watching yachts,
speedboats and the odd brightly
hued pedalo pass by. For a
wilder experience, Bonifacio's
rocky coast is just a 10-minute
drive away.

Fashion first: The dress code is casual
but the sunglasses are always sharp.

Port of call: The beach is in
a protected part of the Gulf of
Sant'Amanza and is a popular spot
for boating. Hire a pedalo or charter
a motor boat to see the surf from
a different perspective (though the
swimming is the real reason to linger).

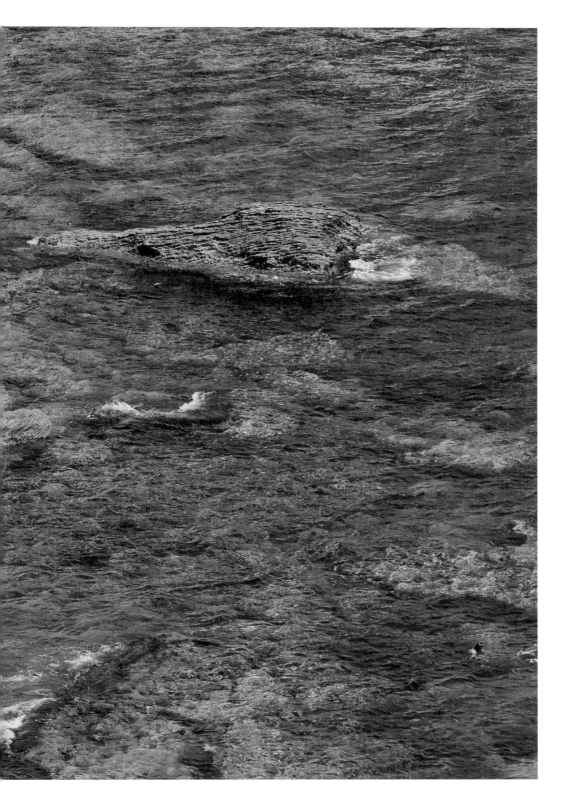

Cascais
Portugal

Straddling the Atlantic Ocean
and Portuguese Riviera,
and a 30-minute commute
from Lisbon, Cascais was
once a holiday retreat for the
Portuguese aristocracy. Today
it is a trendy coastal town with
cobbled streets lined with palm
trees, boutiques and restaurants.
It's also known as the home of
some of Portugal's most scenic
urban beaches. Found along the
Paredão de Cascais coastal path,
each draws a different crowd:
Praia da Duquesa has long
been on the international radar
thanks to its central location but
the smaller Praia das Moitas
is quieter. Nearby Piscina
Oceânica Alberto Romano, a
shallow seawater swimming pool
accessed by wide concrete steps,
invites waders and families.
Striking the balance between
central and sheltered is Praia da
Reigna; a patch of sand that got
its name for being the favourite
spot of Dona Maria Amélia –
Portugal's last queen.

Beach of choice: Portugal's president
Marcelo Rebelo de Sousa lives in
Cascais and enjoys daily swims at
the Praia da Ribeira.

Seaside luxe: The Palácio do Duque
de Loulé overlooks the main beaches
and was a summer residence built in
1873 for a wealthy noble, the second
Duke of Loulé.

Tuba Club
France

More than a few landlocked Parisians and beach-bound Europeans make their way to Marseille's tranquil waters in search of space to unwind in the summer. Those in the know (including France's creative set) will find themselves at Tuba Club in Les Goudes, a pretty fishing village within the Calanques National Park just south of Marseille proper. The five-room hotel, restaurant and bathing spot was revived from the bones of a swimming club that sat here in the 1980s – its name an homage to the former scuba-diving centre. Today it's recognisable by the yellow-and-white-striped sunloungers scattered along the coast, where swirling waters gently lap. An energetic leap or dive into the water from the rocky shore is customary – though there is also a ladder, which allows more discrete swimmers to slip silently into the bracing water. After a few turns (and a few more dives), dry off in the sun and wait for apéro hour when cocktails, such as the playfully named Tuba Libre, begin to flow.

Modest makeover: Architect and designer Marion Mailaender was charged with renovating the space but retaining the spirit of the old diving club. The final design is a riff on Le Corbusier's wooden cabins on the Côte d'Azur.

Dress the part: Tuba Club attracts a fashionable, young crowd so pack your best bikini and swim shorts. Kaftans and straw hats look perfectly at home here.

Seaside selection: The restaurant offers lunch and dinner but bookings are hard to come by. La Marine des Goudes, a five-minute walk away, serves seafood dishes at an unbeatable location above the marina.

Bagno Marino Archi
Italy

While many of the beaches around Salento – the southern tip of Puglia on the very heel of Italy's boot – are long and sandy affairs, this *bagno* (beach club) nestled on Santa Cesarea Terme's cliff-face feels much more dramatic. Don't be put off by the rugged surroundings: various step-ladders lead straight past the rocks so that swimmers can plunge easily into the turquoise sea. An azure raft bobs along in the middle of this private bay and is beloved by those who enjoy diving into the deep waters. The floating platform is also big enough for sunbathers trying to steer clear of the splashes. Above, on a concrete terrace that overlooks the coastline, a restaurant serves fish specials and light pizzas.

Treat yourself: As the "Terme" in the town's name suggests, this area of Puglia is well known for its spa complex, Terme di Santa Cesarea, where treatments with thermal mud are particularly popular. There's also a warm, sulphur-rich pool with a view to the sea.

Hot spot: The best place to recline at this *bagno* is on a secluded platform on the rocky outcrop to the side of the bay. You can enjoy more privacy here.

Sky Lagoon
Iceland

Icelanders are well-known for making the most of the island's geothermal waters. The bathing obsession here dates back to the ninth century, when early settlers used the country's lagoons as a means to survive and recuperate from the brutal weather. In fact, a post-work dip is a national institution and many locals can't fathom life without swimming (or simply wallowing) in hot thermal water. This might be why the country (with a population of only 370,000) has 138 thermal pools. Our pick is the Sky Lagoon, which opened in 2021. The rugged basin is built into the promontory of Kópavogur, a small town that lies south of Reykjavík, and mirrors the country's natural pools. The water is usually a balmy 38C, with sheets of steam almost, but not quite, obscuring views of Snæfellsjökull, a 700,000-year-old glacier-capped stratovolcano. After floating peacefully in the lagoon, make a quick nip to the stone plunge pool and jump into the invigorating (and chilly) 10C depths. You'll almost certainly receive nods of approval from your fellow bathers.

Spa ritual: The infinity pool is one of multiple facilities at the Sky Lagoon. The others include a sauna, steam and mist room.

Dip and sip: In Iceland, baths function as a bar might, offering a daily socialising point. Don't worry, the Sky Lagoon offers both. Once you're finished in the comforting waters, head to the bar to quaff an Icelandic beer.

Cagliari
Italy

Sardinia's salt-kissed capital feels like both a bustling city and laidback beach town – and unlike anywhere else in Italy. Cagliari lies in a wide, sandy bay facing the coast of Tunisia and is closer to Africa than the Italian mainland. It also offers visitors their pick of beautiful beaches. A short drive from the city centre is Poetto Beach, which stretches for nearly 8km and is one of the largest in a European city. A century ago, a tram would bring bathers to the various lidos along the sandy shore. Today restaurants, kiosks and beach clubs dot the strand, which has retained much of its old-world charm. On the other side of the peninsula is the more secluded Spiaggia Calamosca. Typically quieter than the sweeping Poetto, the cove is protected from the island's sometimes harsh winds and offers swimmers calm, clear waters. Cala Fighera, meanwhile, is a favourite of those in the know: this tiny, rocky inlet is hidden from view – perhaps the reason it's so popular with nude bathers. A steep gravel path leads beach-goers to the secret cove, the emerald waters their reward.

Getting there: It takes all of 15 minutes to reach the heart of Cagliari by train from Elmas International Airport, making this one of the most accessible seaside cities to visit.

Spotted: Parco Molentargius natural park sits behind Poetto beach and is among the best spots in Cagliari to see rare birds, including flamingos.

Blown away: It gets windy on Poetto Beach so check the weather before you go. Calamosca and Fighera offer more shelter.

Hydra
Greece

Greece counts more than 2,000 islands scattered around the Mediterranean but few have perfected the balance between pristine deep-blue waters and quality of life as well as Hydra. An hour and a half south of Athens by ferry, the island has forged a community of painters, adventurers and authors over the years who gather here to soak in the sun and visit the numerous exhibitions and galleries that pop up for the warmer season. To enjoy this spot, you'll have to rely on your feet or an affable sea taxi as there are no vehicles on the island (not even bicycles). The quietness of the place and its slow pace extends to some of its beach bars and secluded coves. For a quick dip in the Saronic Gulf, stop at Spilia beach bar or Hydroneta, a few minutes walk from the port, or take a pine-covered path down to Avlaki's pebbled beach for a sunset swim.

Mind your feet: The island's shoreline is dotted with stone and concrete platforms equipped with ladders, so pack appropriate footwear.

Don't miss: The Miaoulia Festival celebrates the anniversary of Greek War of Independence every June. A hand-built wooden boat, packed with fireworks, is set on fire outside the harbour and celebrations go on throughout the night.

Bagno Quattro Venti
Italy

The sandy coast of Emilia-Romagna is where the ideal of the Italian *bagno* was solidified in the 1960s. Here, the flat, straight littoral is parcelled out into a succession of beach clubs that go on uninterrupted for kilometres. The Riviera Romagnola – a 90km stretch on the country's east coast – combines some of Italy's most popular summer nightclubs with child-friendly aqua parks for an atmosphere of light-hearted revelry. The town of Cesenatico, and Bagno Quattro Venti in particular, is a perfect example of this: the beach here is so wide that umbrellas and beds are less crammed together than elsewhere in the country (there's even room for volleyball courts) and the shallow, calm waters of the Adriatic welcome splashing children and adults. The main attraction, though, is Bagno Quattro Venti's dramatic double slide, which catapults swimmers into the air at high-speed.

Keeping score: The *calcio balilla* (foosball table) is an essential feature of many a seaside *bagno*, etched into the holiday memories of many Italians. Both children and adults get extremely competitive during tournaments.

Listen: The Adriatic coast has long been a place where young people go dance; to get in a delightfully retro mood, try listening to Fred Bongusto's 1964 hit "*Una Rotonda Sul Mare*".

Hotel Les Roches Rouges
France

Hotel Les Roches Rouges was made for swimmers. The striking modernist structure was built on the edge of the French Riviera in the 1950s but opened as a smart hotel in 2017 with three bathing opportunities: a 30-metre lap pool, a stone-hewn sea pool and the open Mediterranean. Whether you want to start the day with energetic strokes, cool off in calm water or snorkel in search of marine life, the hotel caters to all. Crisp white sunloungers line the terrace where the sound of lapping waves can be heard and there are endless views of the sea. Don't miss the poolside bar, where negroni provençals are made with Rinquinquin, a local peach apéritif – it's the recommended refreshment before diving back in.

Wine and dine: The poolside bar is open all day. For a taste of Provence, book a table at Récif, the hotel's Michelin-starred restaurant.

Choose your adventure: Discover the surrounding coastline with use of the hotel's paddleboards, kayak and snorkelling equipment. For activities on dry land, hike into the Massif de l'Esterel mountains – its rocky façade's red-hue is the inspiration for the hotel's name.

Belmond Reid's Palace
Portugal

Reid's Palace on the island of
Madeira tops the list of the best
hotel pools with three gems.
Opened in 1891, this baby-pink
construction on a cliff above the
Atlantic was built by Scotsman
William Reid and his sons,
before being acquired by a family
of wine merchants. Now part of
the Belmond luxury hospitality
group, the hotel's British
connection is still apparent:
there are well-tended lawns
surrounding the two main heated
pools and tea is served by waiters
in bow ties, who deftly carry
tiered trays of sandwiches across
marble floors on the terrace.
When guests want to sneak away
for a mellow swim, however,
a lesser-known stone staircase
leads you down the cliffside to an
ocean bath and bathing platform,
with only the waves for company.

Ocean view: Take a chance and dip
into the Atlantic for one of this hotel's
best-kept secrets. When it was built
guests would arrive by boat, so its
frontage was designed to be on the side
facing the water. A swim off the coast
will reveal its true splendour and offer
a chance to admire its architecture just
as William Reid first intended.

Warmer climes: In the era of the
grand ocean liner, Reid's Palace hosted
guests such as Winston Churchill and
playwright George Bernard Shaw who
came to Madeira to restore their health
during the island's mild winter months.

Bagno Sirena
Italy

Plenty of cities around the Mediterranean are set along the sea but many of their urban beaches consist of overcrowded stretches near industrial ports. The Gulf of Naples may be criss-crossed by ferries but head down from the city centre towards the rarefied neighbourhood of Posillipo and the coast transforms into a craggy succession of small rocky coves. Nestled in one of them, just past the genteel Palazzo Donn'Anna, is Bagno Sirena. Its green sunbeds and umbrellas are squeezed into a small, shielded patch of beach. If you'd prefer not to get your feet sandy, there's a wooden pontoon that extends into the water. The restaurant serves more than the *bagno* classic of *fritto misto*, offering anything from fresh grouper to squid-ink risotto and, of course, spaghetti alle vongole on its cheerful painted ceramic plates. It's an enviable lunch spot complete with Mount Vesuvius and Capri at the horizon.

People's palace: Construction for Palazzo Donn'Anna, the building towering over this small beach, began in the 17th century. The untimely death of its eponymous owner meant it was never completed. Over the years, it has served as a crystal factory and a hotel; today it is divided up into private residences.

Day to night: Most *bagni* around Italy – including this one – have hot showers on site so there's no need to head home to get changed at the end of the day if you want to stick around for an aperitivo and dinner.

2.
In the city

More of us than ever now live in cities and so, by default, more of us are also swimming in cities. Savvy urban planners have initiated a wave of regeneration projects that have seen once-unswimmable rivers and lakes transformed into inner-city oases and, along with lidos and public pools, they are increasingly becoming places that people meet, take time out and reconnect with nature. Residents of certain forward-thinking cities no longer need to hop on a plane or pack-up a car to enjoy the benefits of plunging into water. From Switzerland's lakeside clubs and Denmark's harbour baths to the lap pools of Australia, here are our favourite urban bathing spots across the globe.

Havnebadet
Denmark

When the mercury rises, the Danes know how to cool off. Havnebadet (harbour bath) in Aarhus is a timber pool structure designed by Bjarke Ingels in collaboration with urbanist Jan Gehl. The dockside complex, Bassin 7, sits among cranes and shipping containers and comprises two large pools – one rectangular and one circular – as well as two plunge pools and saunas. The floating creation is open year-round but it comes into its own during the summer when children backflip from diving boards, pensioners cut laps in the central pool and students soak up the sun across its many decks.

Urban renewal: Since the baths opened in 2018, the once-industrial area has been transformed by the arrival of apartment blocks, shops and cafés.

Make a splash: There are plenty of opportunities to get on the water – paddleboarding, wakeboarding and waterskiing shops line the harbour.

Prince Alfred Park Pool
Australia

Even in the inner city, Sydneysiders are well served by top swimming spots. On the edge of the once-gritty but now hip neighbourhood of Surry Hills, and conveniently behind the city's Central Station, is the Prince Alfred Park Pool. The space, which houses a 50-metre lap pool and splash pad for toddlers, was given a fresh look in 2013 by Neeson Murcutt Architects, who worked to revitalise the tired area. Today, smart wood-panelled changing rooms flank one side of the pool and a kiosk is on hand for a post swim pick-me-up. On any given day you'll find swimmers of all shapes and sizes chasing each other up and down the lengths. In the fast lane it's Australian crawl (freestyle) while at the slower end elderly ladies in swimming caps crane their necks above the water, breast-stroking down the pool. The grassy surrounds, imagined by landscape architect Sue Barnsley Design, and tiered concrete levels are often dotted with locals and university students sprawled out under the neatly arranged yellow parasols.

Past life: The Prince Alfred Park was named after Queen Victoria's second son who visited Sydney in the 1860s.

Artistic soul: Once the garment district of Sydney, Surry Hills is now a popular haunt for young creatives.

Sai Wan Swimming Shed
Hong Kong

Down a set of concrete steps just beyond Kennedy Town is Sai Wan Swimming Shed – the last of its kind in Hong Kong. There are spartan changing cabins and a spindly pier from which hardy swimmers get a glimpse of the Sulphur Channel. Sampans and ferries sail past, carrying commuters to and from the city's outer islands. Swimming in the choppy water here is not for the faint-hearted and it's advisable to tread carefully; even confident bathers can feel a little timid the first time they follow the narrow boardwalk and leap into the waves. Signs warn of unpredictable currents but venturing out 20 metres and spinning north is far enough to reward bathers with spectacular views of the vertiginous city centre. By mid-morning the pier is usually teeming with swimmers in bright bathing caps – a noticeably senior crowd, looking fit and distinctly fresh.

Bright idea: Invest in a colourful cap like a local. While headwear is not required in all of Hong Kong's swimming spots, it pays to be visible in the open water – and we always support dressing the part.

Be prepared: Pack water and a post-dip snack; this is one of the rare spots on Hong Kong Island without a 7/Eleven or other convenience store close at hand.

The art of exploring: Stroll along the Belcher Bay Promenade, which features art installations and a community garden, after a swim.

The Beverly Hills Hotel
USA

Given all that's happened poolside at The Beverly Hills Hotel – a longstanding bolthole for stars seeking privacy in Los Angeles, where Faye Dunaway sought refuge after winning her first Oscar – it's not surprising that the place retains the atmosphere of a hideaway. The pool at the "Pink Palace" opened in 1938, when sand was trucked in from Arizona to create the sense of a beach club. That space has long gone but its spirit lives on in the unspoken dressiness that's expected of pool guests. In 2021, the 11 private cabanas received a spruce-up by Champalimaud Design, which leaned on the heritage of old Hollywood. So much here has served as the backdrop to the grand old days of Los Angeles, including the striped loungers that have inspired numerous imitations and the much-loved pool managers in white polo shirts and shorts.

Secret access: You have to be a hotel guest to take a dip or stretch out on one of the famed green-and-white sunloungers. The poolside Cabana Café, however, is open to all and offers a perfect sunny perch to read the day's papers.

Guest list: It's said that Leonard Bernstein came up with the idea for *West Side Story* in cabana three, while Katherine Hepburn is said to have once dived into the water fully clothed.

No pictures, please: Refreshingly, taking photographs around the pool is not allowed. Other establishments take note.

Flussbad Oberer Letten
Switzerland

Outdoor swimming is a way of life in Zürich. In the summer, residents dive into their favourite *badis* (swimming clubs) to get in a couple of laps before work, on their lunch breaks and come evening. While most of the city's *badis* are lakeside, Flussbad Oberer Letten is perched on the banks of the River Limmat in the heart of Zürich. The *flussbad* (river pool) was designed by architect couple Elsa and Ernst Burckhardt-Blum in 1952 and features a two-metre-high diving platform and 400-metre-long swimming channel. Wooden decking and concrete bathing areas line the banks and in the summer fill with young sunseekers, drinking and listening to music. The main draw of Oberer Letten, however, is its racing current: the water here is fast – and fun. Bathers jump into the river, get propelled along the waterway and hop out further downstream – only to run back and do it all again.

Splashing around: The annual Limmat-Schwimmen event ends at Oberer Letten, where thousands of swimmers pass by on colourful rubber inflatables.

Aquatic bygones: There's been a bathing establishment at the Letten since 1896; in the beginning it was only a simple wooden construction.

Dip in: If you're peckish, trot up the stairs to Panama Bar for a bite to eat or a post-swim Aperol spritz. Customers still wet from the river are welcome.

Amalienbad
Austria

When Amalienbad opened in 1926 it was one of Europe's largest public baths. An art nouveau marvel that could hold up to 1,300 visitors, it was built as part of a push by Vienna's city council to encourage fitness and personal hygiene at a time when many city dwellers lacked bathrooms. Today it remains much loved by a new generation of Viennese who head here to perfect their backstroke while admiring the elegant ceiling. The building stands on the site of the ancient Roman baths in a complex designed by architects Karl Schmalhofer and Otto Nadel. Amalienbad was bombed during the Second World War and the building was restored in the 1980s. The original glass ceiling, which once opened to allow air into the room, was also destroyed. While it has been beautifully reconstructed, the sliding panels haven't opened since.

Plan ahead: The pool is closed on Mondays and its opening times vary throughout the week.

Getting steamy: Aside from the main pool, Amalienbad has a steam bath and cold plunge pool. It also has three saunas, one for nude bathers. Consult the timetable before barging in, though – there are specific times for mixed, male and female bathing.

Sporting Club
Lebanon

Every summer, Beirut becomes a city of beach-goers and sun-worshippers – even through the city's most tumultuous times. One of the oldest and best-known places to take a dip is Sporting Club, a family-run joint that opened in 1953 and quickly became the place to seek politicians and film stars alike. The spot has since morphed from a shack on the rocks to a 10,000 sq m institution with three pools, a squash court, kayak and paddleboard hire, sunbathing platforms and a restaurant and café that serve excellent seafood. Plastic loungers, ageing locker rooms and metal-framed canopies somehow make it all the more charming, while the intergenerational clientele helps make Sporting what it is. On the hottest days of the year, expect to navigate old timers playing backgammon, gaggles of students bronzing their bodies, fishermen trying their luck and intellectuals trading politics for a glass of *arak* under the sun.

High life: On Friday and Saturday nights, Sporting hosts epic parties where revellers can drink and dance as the waves crash on the rocks below.

Nice refuge: Even during the 1975 to 1990 civil war, residents would take advantage of lulls in the fighting to swim in the sea and sunbathe.

Swim with a view: Sporting also has a wonderful view of the city's iconic Pigeon's Rock, a naturally formed arch jutting out of the sea just off the western coast. Mostly, however, the Sporting view is of concrete, orange awnings and the sea (but there is no beach as such).

Gordon Pool
Israel

At 06.00 every weekday morning Gordon Pool on Tel Aviv's seafront opens to loyal bathers who start their day with a dip in its salty waters. The complex originally opened in 1956 with the aim to create a clean bathing spot away from the untreated waste that flowed into the sea at the time. Every evening at 21.00 pool staff empty the three basins (including a 50-metre lap pool) into the Mediterranean Sea. A thorough cleaning ensues and then custom-built pumps extract ground-water from two wells to refill the baths for the next day. Thanks to this system, the water remains clean, mineral-rich and at a constant year-round temperature of 24C. Gordon pool has around 4,000 members and it allows walk-ins too, so on a summer day the wooden decking is teeming with young sunseekers, office workers and grey-haired pensioners all mingling together. Visitors be warned: Gordon Pool is a place for serious swimming, so strap on your goggles and join the locals as they breaststroke down the orderly lanes.

Getting there: The swimming pool overlooks Tel Aviv's marina and is easy to reach from the centre of the city, whether on foot, by bike or car.

Refreshing change: This Tel Aviv institution underwent thorough renovations in 2009, which saw the original 1956 complex updated to include pools for children and toddlers as well as a modern wooden deck with sunbeds and chairs.

Gänsehäufel
Austria

Summer days in Vienna are often spent on Gänsehäufel – an island on the Old Danube, an inactive arm of the river – where you'll find a cross-section of Austrian society idly passing the time. Twenty minutes on the metro from Vienna's centre, this vast wooded space is an urban haven with lawns, lakeside beaches, pools and other places to beat the heat. From early May to mid-September, anyone can come to splash about on its sandy shores and in its multiple pools, play beach volleyball or cycle around the island. Young Viennese families can also enjoy the shallow lido, which is one of the longest in Europe. There's opportunity to lounge and swim au naturel in the nudist area – a popular fixture since the 1980s. Whatever you seek from the Austrian summer, you will find it here.

Storied past: Gänsehäufel was damaged in the Second World War and was reimagined by architects Max Fellerer, Carl Appel and Eugen Wörle in the late 1940s. Today it is a modernist marvel of clean lines and sweeping concrete curves.

All in the name: The island is named for the goose breeding (*gänse* are geese, *häufel* is a small river embankment) that traditionally took place on the site.

Quiet zone: The island is family friendly but, if you prefer to evade splashing and squeals, migrate to the calmer northern end.

Kennedy Town Swimming Pool
Hong Kong

When Hong Kong's subway operator wanted to knock down Kennedy Town's old swimming pool to make room for a new station, it was first required to build a new one. The result is one of the city's most picturesque places to take a plunge – other than the nearby Sai Wan Swimming Shed (*see page 96*). The modern landmark was designed by internationally-renowned architecture firm Farrells, most famous in Hong Kong for its curved viewing platform at the top of Peak Tower. Inside Kennedy Town Swimming Pool's silvery curved exterior are four pools – opt for the outdoor lap pool which boasts views of Victoria Harbour and (if you decide to swim backstroke) the city's distinctive high-rise housing. Be mindful of the early-morning crowds, when lanes can be as chaotic as the city's pavements and laps are performed in artistic zig zags. Swimming is a social exercise in Hong Kong, so don't be surprised to see groups of seniors huddled in the shallow end, chatting while perfecting synchronised movements.

Choice laps: Hong Kong is well served by public swimming pools with low entrance fees.

Flex time: Stretching is serious business here. Limber up on the pool deck while looking out across Victoria Harbour.

Cash in: Remember to bring a HK$5 (€0.60) coin for the lockers or change a note with the friendly staff at the entrance.

Copenhagen
Denmark

In Copenhagen, you're never far from water: the city has 10 designated bathing zones where swimming is permitted day and night, and the water quality is checked regularly. The harbour baths include Islands Brygge, the city's most visited; Fisketorvet, for serious lap swimmers; and Sluseholmen, which boasts two pools and a lagoon-like space. Many of the zones are designed with fun in mind: Kalvebod Bølge in the Vesterbro district is a visual representation of its name – "*bølge*" means "wave" in Danish – and features undulating bridges that Copenhageners leap from in the summer. Kastrup Sea Bath in Øresund Sound is known by locals as "The Snail" because of its circular wooden form, the curved deck sloping into a five-metre-high platform poised for jumping off of. For a more relaxed experience, the city also has a number of nearby sandy beaches: locals favour Bellevue, Hellerup and Amagar or Charlottenlund Søbad – one of Denmark's oldest *badeklub* (swimming clubs).

Safety first: Stick to the official bathing zones – the water quality is monitored and there's no risk of getting in the way of a ship. The city introduced fines for illegal swimming outside the designated areas in 2021.

Scrubbed up: Copenhagen's first harbour bath opened in 2002 following a decade-long clean-up programme. Copenhageners now flock to the baths which are open to all in summer, but become members-only in the winter.

Piscina Municipal
de Montjuïc
Spain

Sitting high on the sides of
Montjuïc hill in Barcelona,
Piscina Municipal de Montjuïc
was built in 1929, refurbished
for the 1955 Mediterranean
Games and expanded for the
1992 Olympics. Today, it attracts
professional swimmers, divers
and a parade of lithe bodies
hoping to work on their tans.
Kylie Minogue fans will know
it as the spot where the singer
filmed the video for her 2003
hit single "Slow". In the opening
shot, a Speedo-clad diver
somersaults in slow motion from
the pool's 10-metre-high board;
behind him is a panorama of the
Barcelona skyline and Collserola
mountains beyond. These views
have helped make the municipal
pool one of the Catalan capital's
most popular swimming spots.
Although it's said that Spaniards
start their days later than most,
the chance to nab a sunny spot
here has them queueing from
the early morning. It's open for
public use in the summer when
it fills up quickly with bathers
looking for a refreshing escape
from the heat.

Sitting pretty: As part of the
renovations for the 1992 Olympics,
6,500 spectator seats were added and
many are still staggered up the hill
facing the Barcelona skyline.

Top of the town: Opposite the pool
is a cable car station where you can
catch a ride to the viewing point at the
top of Montjuïc.

Palma Sport & Tennis Club
Spain

Opened in 1964, Mallorca's Palma Sport & Tennis Club and its latticed rationalist building became an instant hit with the city's high society, with many of its members eager to outdo their peers on the central clay court. This was exactly the spirit of neighbourly sportsmanship that Swedish hospitality entrepreneurs Mikael and Johanna Landström wanted to recreate when they bought the dilapidated spot in 2013, promising to restore the sporting club to its glamorous heyday. The pair added a sleek gym, launched the Legends' Cup tennis tournament and revamped the swimming pool, which today gives the complex its splashing heart. The five-lane lap pool may place fitness before a leisurely dip, but that doesn't mean you won't catch plenty of slender locals lounging around its Nak sunbed-lined edges. Balancing good-spirited competition, social connection and laidback style, this well-heeled sports club pool is a modern community watering hole. From early-morning fitness to lazy afternoons spent under the sun or shade, everyone has a place here.

Art trail: Soak up the eye-catching collection of sculpture installations scattered around the grounds, all sourced by Swedish art dealer Stephan Lundgren.

Fitness first: The lower-level gym, with its exposed concrete, offers around 200 weekly group classes. The spa's Turkish, Finnish and infra-red saunas work wonders for tennis-weary muscles – as does a healthy stretch in the sun.

Rhine River
Switzerland

The deep thrum of cargo ships bound for Rotterdam vibrate the air as they move up the Rhine River in Basel, while groups of swimmers happily float along undisturbed by the ruckus. Thousands of people swim through the Swiss city every year, bobbing past restaurants, wooden fishing huts, shops and museums. Families spread out on concrete steps, while sunbathers relax on gravel-shored islands and the wooden decking at the Rheinbad Breite (a popular bathing platform). This idyllic scene was not always thus: in the 1980s the river wasn't fit for swimming but things improved dramatically following legislation and a dedicated focus on its clean-up. Basel brought people back to the water with cultural events, a redesign and rewilding of the river's edges and, of course, the promise of a good spritz.

High and dry: Before entering the cool water tuck your belongings into a colourful waterproof bag that doubles as a tow float.

Food to go: The river has become a lunchtime conduit with swimmers paddling to the city centre to pick up something to eat. Friendly staff will expertly wrap your snack so it'll survive the swim back.

Sight swimming: The Rhine's waterside highlights include the mid-century power station Kraftwerk Birsfelden and Roche Tower by Herzog & de Meuron.

Swimming Stadium
Finland

Finns love to swim and almost every Finnish city boasts several pools – albeit mostly indoor spaces due to the country's chilly climate. The legendary Swimming Stadium, or more familiarly Stadikka, in Helsinki is the oldest public outdoor complex in Finland. The four pools – one Olympic, one for diving, one for wading and another for children – are nestled among spruces, greenery and low cliffs just a few streets from the centre. Many of those who remain in the city for the summer see the stadium as a convenient way to make the most of warmer days. It's easy to spend an entire day here, lounging on wooden benches or the surrounding lawn, reading, playing basketball and, of course, swimming. There's a rite of passage that all visitors should try: the long climb to the top of the tallest diving board. Springing off the 10-metre level earns you the most points among Helsinkians but, if that's too daunting, there's no shame in settling for the five or three-metre boards. Before you dive, don't forget to take in the sweeping views from the top.

False start: The complex was designed by architect Jorma Järvi ahead of the 1940 Winter Olympics, which was cancelled because of the Second World War. It did eventually get its time in the spotlight, when it hosted the aquatic races in the 1952 summer event.

Jumping funny: One of the Stadikka's annual attractions is a clown diving competition, where fancy-dress-clad swimmers leap into the air to the glee of the cheering crowd below.

Bäderquartier
Switzerland

Some like it hot, some like it cold – postcard-pretty Baden in Switzerland offers both. Here, the cool, rapid-flowing River Limmat runs through the town, while warm geothermal waters bubble up from beneath. Baden's bathing heyday was in the early 20th century, when people would flock here to sample the area's supposedly curative waters. Eventually, Baden's baths closed after decades of neglect. Now, though, the town has returned to the water with its Bäderquartier (bathing quarter) comprised of three thermal baths – two public and one private. The latter is Fortyseven spa complex, which was designed by Mario Botta and gets its name from the temperature of the mineral-rich water. The public baths are Heisse Brunnen Baden and Heisse Brunnen Ennetbaden, which sit on either side of the river. The areas have three stone pools each of varying sizes and temperatures – the smallest remains a toasty 42C while the largest is a comfortable 36C. The baths enjoy a friendly competition: the Ennetbaden side is arguably prettier, set under old chestnut trees, while Baden is bigger and livelier – it is no stranger to a popped cork or a late-night dip.

Crowning glory: Fortyseven's building is 160-metres long and sits above the revived Bäderquartier with pools that glow by night and steam by day.

Get sporty: If the baths draw a diverse crowd, so does the River Limmat, where a slalom course is popular with kayakers and surfers.

Széchenyi Thermal Bath
Hungary

Straddling a geological fault line has its benefits: Budapest is home to more than 100 thermal springs that have been used for bathing since Roman times. This mineral-rich water is said to possess all sorts of healing properties and wallowing in it is an important part of local culture, earning Budapest the moniker "City of Spas". The largest is Széchenyi, which is made up of 15 indoor baths and three grand outdoor pools. The vibrant yellow, neo-baroque complex was designed by architect Gyozo Czigler and opened in the heart of Budapest City Park in 1913. It was named after Count Istvan Széchenyi, whose various initiatives (including the building of the first bridge between Buda and Pest) helped turn the city into a flourishing metropolis. Today, the baths that bear his name are an important meeting point for locals of all ages to gossip, sunbathe and play chess on concrete platforms in the water.

Annual appeal: These thermal baths are open year-round and are filled with visitors and locals enjoying the warm waters even as snowflakes fall around them in winter.

Big hit: "Sparties" take place here on Saturday nights, with colourful light shows and live DJ sets. They tend to be rather raucous affairs.

North Sydney Olympic Pool
Australia

Sitting pretty on Milsons Point is the North Sydney Olympic Pool, with an unbeatable view of the Sydney Harbour Bridge and the yellow and green ferries transporting Sydneysiders between the North Shore and the CBD. Flanked by the bridge and the grinning entrance to the 1930s-built Luna Park funfair, the pool opened in 1936 just in time for the 1938 Empire Games (renamed the Commonwealth Games). The art deco marvel, with its colourful shells and marine-themed masonry, boasts a 50-metre, nine-lane pool. Since opening, the site has seen 86 world swimming records set by legendary Australians including Lorraine Crapp, Shane Gould and siblings Jon and Ilsa Konrads.

Changing lanes: Serious swimmers frown on those lingering in the water here. Anyone performing slower, non-front-crawl strokes should avoid the fast lane.

Looking good: Make your way to nearby Milsons Point lookout in Bradfield Park for stunning views of the city, especially Sydney Opera House across the harbour.

Belmond Copacabana Palace
Brazil

From Brigitte Bardot and Luciano Pavarotti, to heads of state and royalty, the Belmond Copacabana Palace – and its pool – has welcomed a highly illustrious set of guests since it opened its doors in 1923. As Rio de Janeiro's oldest hotel, it has also hosted some wild parties. Although the surroundings are undeniably grand, the beautiful outdoor pool is a distinctly relaxed affair. Supervised day and night, it is discreet, understated and instantly welcoming. In the morning, the 25-metre pool is filled with serious swimmers racking up laps. Come lunchtime, it's a much more sedate affair: visitors gently cool off in the water while many enjoy a poolside lunch – with lots of caipirinhas on the side. Guests quickly learn which sunbeds stay in the sun the longest – make sure you're one of them.

Walk of fame: The hotel has ushered in a roster of renowned guests since its opening: Édith Piaf once serenaded customers, the king and queen of Norway laid their heads on its pillows and the Rolling Stones used one of the grand hallways as a running track before performing on Copacabana Beach in 2006.

Life's a beach: Take advantage of the hotel's beach service where all your seaside paraphernalia is set up for you. It includes cold face towels and a watering can to keep your feet cool.

Taste of Rio: Sample Brazilian beach snacks at the palace. Try local favourite *dadinhos de tapioca*, fried cubes of tapioca stuffed with cheese.

Bagni Misteriosi
Italy

A 1930s gem set among the densely packed apartment buildings of Porta Romana, the twin pools of Milan's Bagni Misteriosi put architecture to the fore, which seems fitting in Italy's city of design. Opened in 1937 as the Piscine Caimi, the pools were created by Lorenzo Secchi to celebrate leisure. He placed a sculpture of three flamingos in the middle of the water as an ode to Italy's classical fountains. After years of abandonment, the pools underwent a 2015 redevelopment by esteemed architect Michele de Lucchi, which restored them to their full glory. Bagni Misteriosi remains the best place to enjoy a swim and see the Milanese at play as they sprawl on the grass or take a dip during Lombardy's steamy summers.

Aperitivo hour: Enjoy the scene with a drink at the poolside bar, which livens up in the late afternoon.

Under the sun: There's little shade for bathers, so pack suncream and a wide-brimmed straw hat, preferably from Borsalino or Milan's Melegari, to fit in with the city's stylish denizens.

Setting the stage: Overlooked by the neighbouring Franco Parenti theatre, the pools also function as outdoor platforms hosting performances, markets and festivals.

Le Bassin de la Villette
France

Along the Quai de la Loire, in
the 19th arrondissement in Paris,
this unexpected swimming hole
is bursting with life. Residents
tend to flee for sandier shores
in the summer before the heat
and crowds descend on the city.
Le Bassin de la Villette – or
rather the lake's bathing area
– is an anchor that keeps folk
around. The French capital is a
champion of urban swimming:
in 2002 it launched Paris Plages,
a project that transforms the
city with pop-up beaches and
swimming spots in July and
August every year. Le Bassin de
la Villette's floating pool was a
welcome addition in 2017, built
as part of mayor Anne Hidalgo's
"Nager à Paris" (swimming in
Paris) scheme with the aim to
clean up the city's waterways
for the 2024 Summer Olympics.
The complex, which comprises
three pools that bob beside
the leafy riverbank, returns
every summer. The pools and
adjacent lawn, often scattered
with colourful deckchairs, have
become a popular spot and an
inspiring piece of urbanism,
connecting Parisians to water
in their city.

In supply: Le Bassin de la Villette
is the largest artificial lake in Paris
and was formed in 1808 as a reserve
for drinking water. Before the 19th
century, the area was dedicated to
gardens and public space.

Cultural hit: A five-minute walk
from the pools is the Cent Quatre,
a factory-turned-cultural centre
that hosts concerts, performances
and exhibitions.

Les Bains des Docks
France

France's historic port city of Le Havre rose from the rubble of the Second World War to become a paean to modernism. While the city is busy restoring its past, it is also keen to add to its architectural legacy. In the early 2000s, it invested €22m in a stunning white stucco and ceramic swimming complex designed by Pritzker-prize winning French architect Jean Nouvel as part of a redevelopment of the area's docklands. Hidden behind an unassuming black façade, the stark cubic site includes an Olympic-sized open-air pool and 11 interconnecting indoor-outdoor baths (the latter inspired by natural rockpools, each one linked to the next), a spa and fitness centre.

In hot water: The complex is open year-round. In the winter, the outdoor pools can be accessed through heated swimming channels.

Global appeal: Architect Jean Nouvel has designed buildings around the world, from the pavilion which houses Jane's Carousel in Brooklyn to the National Museum of Qatar in Doha, completed in 2019.

Space to explore: The surrounding dockland area is full of bars and restaurants, with the city's Museum of Modern Art André Malraux within walking distance.

Gellért Thermal Bath
Hungary

From Ottoman occupation
to the heights of the Austro-
Hungarian empire, Budapest's
residents and rulers have long
sought out a good soak. Today
that translates to an enviable
selection of spas, or *fürdo*. The
best-known is the palatial,
sprawling Széchenyi Thermal
Bath (*see page 138*). A lower-
key alternative is the Gellért
Thermal Bath – part of the
hotel of the same name – which
features a top-lit courtyard
pool, an outdoor pool, brass
bannisters and extravagant
art nouveau tiles throughout.
Don't miss the vintage wave
pool (only open in the summer)
and the spa: there are six saunas
heated at increasingly sweltering
temperatures as well as two
steam rooms. A dip in the icy
plunge pool completes the
Hungarian experience.

Bath time: People have been taking
to the waters at Gellért for centuries.
There were baths at the site during
the Ottoman era – and references to
its healing powers date back to the
13th century.

Meet and steep: While the baths
have become a popular tourist haunt,
you'll also find locals socialising and
soaking here while there's often a
gaggle of older Hungarian men who
have gathered to talk politics.

Allas Sea Pool
Finland

Allas Sea Pool in Helsinki's harbour offers a distinct way to experience the city: directly from the water. Begin your visit in the floating complex's saunas – heated every day of the year – before cooling off in the water. There are three pools to choose from, including a seawater pool that uses filtered water pumped in from beyond the harbour, a children's pool and a lap pool. Swimmers can take a few turns with views of the city's presidential palace, or in the shadows of a cruise ship. The popular moonlight swim, meanwhile, allows bathers to admire the city's illuminated waterfront. The lap pool is heated year round and, even when air temperatures plunge below zero and the sea is covered in ice, you'll find Helsinkians gliding up and down.

Feel the heat: The complex is an engineering feat that uses a combination of heated water and seawater that's pumped, filtered and carried to the site.

Swim sustenance: The pool café is open daily and year round. Book a table at the Allas Seagrill restaurant upstairs or order cocktails on the Allas Sky Bar's roof terrace for something more refined.

Bains des Pâquis
Switzerland

Geneva's much-loved public bathing club sits on the northern front of the city's lake and remains a lively place year-round. A modest jetty is flanked by a beach on one side and a set of single-storey buildings that encompasses sunbathing platforms, a sauna, hammam and restaurant Buvette on the other. The Bains have been public since 1890 but the current rationalist complex was built in 1932 by architect Henry Roche and engineer Louis Archinard. Genevans from all walks of life engage in all manner of pastimes here – from office workers cutting laps in the morning and bronzed students steadily paddleboarding on the water to children leaping from the concrete diving tower. But it's the diehards who make this place what it is: regulars swim here even when ice forms on the water. Visit for fondue on chilly evenings and arrive as dawn breaks in the summer, when live classical music graces the baths at 06:00.

All you can eat: Buvette is the buzzing restaurant. Stop for a bircher-muesli breakfast and to rub shoulders with early-morning swimmers or, come evening, when the restaurant becomes a bustling bar.

Creative licence: The baths regularly host art exhibitions, poetry readings and musical events.

Tahiti Beach Club
Morocco

Casablanca, Morocco's largest city, is a gleaming metropolis of commerce, architecture, nightlife – and beach clubs. The seaside strip, La Corniche, is home to sandy stretches popular with residents and visitors, though the waves are often big and, as a result, brimming with surfers. For a relaxing swim, head to one of the many outposts that line the oceanfront instead. The oldest, and most resilient, is the lively Tahiti Beach Club. First opened as the Tahiti Plage in 1940, this storied spot has three restaurants, eight swimming pools and a well-oiled clientele – and is one of Casablanca's top places to be seen. The blush-coloured paths are pitter-pattered by all manner of Casablancais: families secure sunbeds; smokers chat business around restaurant tables; children leap into the water; and sunglass-wearing youths clamour for cocktails at the bar. This might be an artificial oasis but the playful atmosphere has a natural flow.

Home swim home: Day bungalows provide privacy for Tahiti Beach Club members. They can be booked from May to October.

Play on: A surf school, sports classes and a children's playground keep more active sorts occupied.

The Hollywood Roosevelt
USA

The pool at the Roosevelt has long been the place where Hollywood goes to cool off. In 1929, the LA-based hotel hosted the first-ever Academy Awards and its pool became a firm fixture. The steady sway of the old palm trees still conjures a quiet and easy atmosphere, transporting guests far from hustle beyond the gates. These days, the Roosevelt pool is less a place to learn lines and more of a scene in its own right – especially on Saturdays – with a DJ and an attentive sunbed service at the Tropicana Pool & Café cocktail bar. Although the hotel shows its age a little, the pool comes with perhaps the greatest pedigree: David Hockney painted a mural on the bottom tiles in the 1980s, with aquatic-looking wavy lines that still shimmer under the water today.

Need to know: Day passes for the pool quickly sell out, especially on Saturdays in summer. Book ahead and get there before noon to snag one of the coveted sunbeds.

Picture perfect: During the Felix Art Fair, held every year at the Roosevelt, poolside cabanas become temporary exhibition spaces – great for snapping up pieces, less so for catching rays.

After dark: The open fireplace at the Tropicana Pool & Café is the place to retire to when the sun goes down.

Park Hyatt Tokyo
Japan

In one of the most indelible scenes in Sofia Coppola's now classic film, *Lost in Translation*, a young Scarlett Johansson contemplates Tokyo from the Park Hyatt to the sound of Squarepusher's track "Tommib" before diving into the hotel pool. That same pool is thrillingly situated on the 47th floor in the hotel's spa and fitness centre, Club On the Park (which is only accessible for guests and members). The building was designed by Pritzker-prize winning architect, the late Kenzo Tange, who teamed up with Hong Kong-based US interior designer John Morford to create the room's distinctive steel and glass pyramid roof. There are panoramic views over the city and, on a clear day, you can see as far as Mount Fuji. It's an inspiring sight, particularly in the early morning and early evening, when dusk falls and Tokyo starts to sparkle.

Lap it up: The pool is open from 06.00 to 22.00. Swimmers can sign up for aqua walking classes or technique training for improved stroke style.

Street view: The hotel rises from the 39th to the 52nd floor of a glassy skyscraper in Shinjuku. The iconic vistas of Toyko's cityscape can be seen from every storey.

3.
Lakes and mountains

There's nothing quite like leaping into an invigorating glacial lake or swimming to a floating dock and savouring your reward – the heat of the sun – when you get there. Or swapping the busyness of the city for a hidden hotel where clear waters (and a dose of good design) envelop your body, washing away the thoughts of diaries, dinner plans and duties. In the following pages, we've compiled our favourite outposts with a touch of wilderness – from Alpine lakes to plunge into and rivers where rosé is happily quaffed on the shoreside to cool, calm mountain hotels with nothing but the trees for company.

Lake Cauma
Switzerland

Switzerland is dotted with mountain lakes but few are as beautiful as the emerald-hued Cauma. The lake is the jewel in the crown of Flims, a town known for its extraordinary skiing and hilly vistas, and which offers all the elements of a summer swimming utopia. A two-hour train ride from Zürich, this spot offers a level of remoteness found only in the mountains. A yellow Postbus drops visitors near a funicular that takes them down to the lake where bathers can cool down and switch off (loud phone calls and blaring music are frowned upon here). But the area is not without its comforts: there's a kiosk that sells swimwear and inflatables, and there are lockers, showers and changing rooms, as well as plenty of tree-sheltered banks on which to throw down a towel. On warm days, the shoreline fills with sun worshippers and swimmers, and divers climb to the top of a small rocky outcrop and jump into the glistening water below.

Health kick: Flims was established as a *kurort* (health resort) in the 19th century due to the lake's supposed rejuvenating powers.

Fashion faux pas: Sorry to all the nudists, Cauma has a strict swimsuit policy. If you turn up without, though, you can buy one at the entrance.

Alpine adventure: Take advantage of the Swiss scenery post-dip – the lake is attached to 250km of hiking and biking trails.

Hotel Bavaria
Italy

There's something about Merano's pleasing climate and genteel architecture that dictates a leisurely pace of life. Part medieval stronghold, part Austrian spa, the South Tyrolean town has long been known for its water and treatments. In fact, rest, recuperation and wellbeing have been local specialities since Empress Elisabeth of Austria-Hungary chose to holiday here in the 19th century. The family-run Hotel Bavaria, set in the hills above Merano, follows in this tradition. Built in 1883, the villa's bright blue façade, sweeping white balconies and canary yellow parasols look as though they were dreamt up by Wes Anderson. But an expertly-clipped garden of rose bushes, and cedar, palm and olive trees conceals an Alpine oasis: the pool. After mountain excursions, guests can dip into the azure waters and recline on a striped sunlounger, palm leaves gently rustling in the breeze. There is something of another time here: of simple holiday pleasures and well-earned indulgences.

Merano microclimate: The Texelgruppe mountains protect the area from rain and winds from the north, resulting in particularly mild weather.

Mountain meander: Head into the hills by catching the nearby Merano 2000 cable car, which provides access to hiking trails, lodges and restaurants.

And relax: The area is also home to a large thermal bath complex, Terme Merano, designed by architect Matteo Thun.

Lido di Lugano
Switzerland

Lake Lugano is a freshwater gem between Switzerland and Italy, and Lido di Lugano's wide shallow beach is a prime launch point for a gentle swim. Although the summer climate can feel tropical, the scenery is pure Alpine (aside from a palm tree here and there). The lake's northern bank is where you'll find its namesake town and the historic *badi*, which was designed in 1928 by the city's then-deputy mayor, Americo Marazzi. Not much has changed since: lush lawns and a beach surround the red-timber lake house, which has a round roof emblazoned with "L-I-D-O" front and back – just in case you forget where you are. As well as the glittering natural waters of Lake Lugano, there are four pools to splash about in. The lido welcomes some 4,000 bathers during its midsummer peak but, worry not, there's space for everyone to enjoy the sun, or tuck themselves under its signature green umbrellas.

Snack spot: Food is served at the restaurant at the heart of the *badi*. Its dining area is dotted with red-and-white parasols and a cook can be seen tossing French fries in the air to tempt onlookers. Just steer clear of the lido's resident swan – he'll snatch your chips given the chance.

Sundown activities: After dark, films are shown on a big screen and early-evening concerts fill the air with music.

Don't miss: La Traversata is an annual event in August that sees hundreds of people take part in a 2,500-metre swim in Lake Lugano.

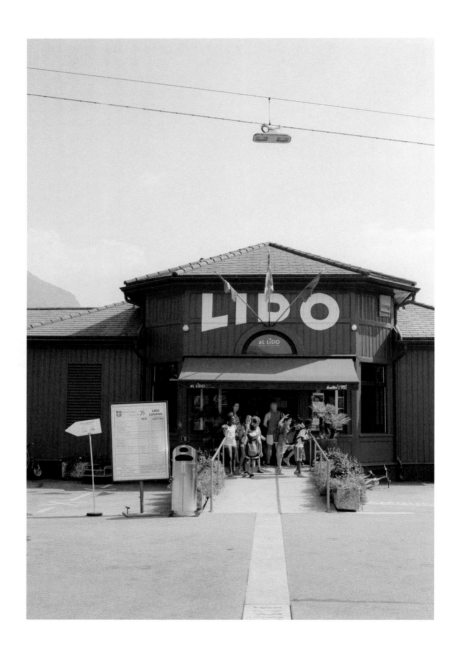

Strandbag Seeburg
Switzerland

In the heat of the summer, the Swiss cool off at lakeside swimming spots, which are as much a cultural motif as they are bathing establishments. Take a short downhill drive from the idyllic village of Küssnacht am Rigi to the edge of Lake Lucerne, where the *strandbad* (lido) has a relaxed vibe. At its peak, Strandbad Seeburg attracts hundreds of visitors every day: swimmers flock past the V-shaped entrance at all hours, towels and umbrellas in hand, to sunbathe on the lawn or jump into the tranquil lake. Its long opening hours help to attract a diverse crowd: the athletic set arrive by 09.00 for a morning swim, families make themselves at home during the day and free entry after 17.00 lures many for a post-work dip and apéro.

New look: Like many of the country's public swimming clubs, this one dates back to the first half of the 20th century. The original structure was replaced with a wooden building in 2009 designed by architecture firm GKS.

Club house: The Badi Seeburg Küssnacht restaurant is open year round and offers fresh salads, burgers and drinks on a sunny terrace. It also hosts live music and art exhibitions.

Easy access: Strandbad Seeburg is just over an hour away from Zürich by train and 45-minutes by car.

Krumme Lanke
Germany

Venture to Berlin's periphery
and you will be rewarded with
swathes of woodland peppered
with secluded lakes. Of the 3,000
that surround the city, Krumme
Lanke is one of the most popular.
The lake is a 30-minute drive
from Berlin's centre, set in the
south-western district of Steglitz-
Zehlendorf. It's a scenic spot
hidden in the deep thickets of
Grunewald forest and makes
for a welcome escape from
the urban buzz of the capital.
There's a 4km boardwalk
surrounding its shores, which
draws joggers and walkers, and
a large meadow at one end
where bathers can lay out their
towels. Come summer, it fills
with everyone from picnicking
families to revellers recovering
from a heavy night at Berghain.
And naturally – this is Germany,
after all – nudist bathing is
allowed at one of Krumme
Lanke's sandy shores.

Ahead of the curve: The name
Krumme Lanke comes from ancient
Middle Low German and means
"crooked lake" in reference to its
twisting shoreline.

Sing it: In 1923, Berlin folk singer
Fredy Sieg wrote "*Das Lied von der
Krummen Lanke*" ("The Song of
Krumme Lanke") which tells a
boy-meets-girl tale set on the banks
of the lake.

By the seasons: The lake is open
year-round. It often freezes over in
the winter, making it a popular
ice-skating destination.

Miramonti
Italy

This South Tyrolean hotel, perched on a 1,200-metre-high cliff, offers swimming with unparalleled views. From the mountain-top spot, the city of Merano looks small in the low valley and hulking white-capped Alpine summits lie ahead. These sweeping vistas are best enjoyed from the hotel's heated infinity pool, which is open year-round – even (or especially) when snow is falling. It is framed by a pitched roof and seems to cantilever over the brink as steam rises towards the clouds. An outdoor observation deck, kitted with recliners, overlooks the serrated peaks of the sierra. Inside the hotel, three restaurants offer Alpine and Mediterranean food, and there's an afternoon cake buffet for those with a sweet tooth.

Soak and see: A few steps into the pinewoods behind the hotel is a hot tub and sleek sauna with views of the forest and mountains.

A to B: The hotel offers a Land Rover shuttle service in all seasons, be it a summer stroll or day of skiing at any of the surrounding resorts.

4.
The places we've swum

Photographs of where we swim are personal. They are infused with memories of sunny days, quiet moments, conversations and seaside meals. Some are vivid moments from unforgettable trips, others fleeting feelings we've tried to capture. In this scrapbook, we present a series of snapshots from the areas that MONOCLE editors have visited, taken a dip at – and loved. These are the locations around the world that bring us joy.

Platja Pou d'es Lleo
Ibiza, Spain

Strandbad Küsnacht
Küsnacht, Switzerland

Miami Beach
Florida, USA

Meisters Hotel Irma
Merano, Italy

Cala Victoria Beach
Mallorca, Spain

Ammos Hotel
Crete, Greece

Cretan Malia Park
Crete, Greece

Rosemary Beach
Florida, USA

Vermentinu Primonte Villa
Corsica, France

Butterfly Valley
Mugla, Turkey

Qasr Al Sarab Desert Resort
Abu Dhabi, UAE

Wild Beach
Antalya, Turkey

Žitna Beach
Korcula, Croatia

Fish Hoek Beach
Cape Town, South Africa

Brancaster Staithe
Norfolk, UK

Stahl House
California, USA

Plage d'Imsouane
Imsouane, Morocco

Kenwood Ladies' Pond
London, UK

Bjørvika
Oslo, Norway

Ham Tin Beach
Tai Long, Hong Kong

Bude Sea Pool
Cornwall, UK

Ross Jones Rockpool
Sydney, Australia

Concepció by Nobis
Mallorca, Spain

Porthcurno Beach
Cornwall, UK

Playa Holbox
Quintana Roo, Mexico

Brockwell Lido
London, UK

Basshaunt Lake
Ontario, Canada

Wadi Ash Shab
Tiwi, Oman

Playa de Illetes
Mallorca, Spain

Lake Zürich
Zürich, Switzerland

Bambu Indah Resort
Bali, Indonesia

Paloma Beach
Saint-Jean-Cap-Ferrat, France

Waikiki Natatorium War Memorial
Hawaii, USA

5.
Essays

There's a whole lot more to swimming than, well, swimming. From leaping and lapping to tentatively toe-dipping, it means something different to everyone. We asked writers, thinkers and MONOCLE editors to reflect on this popular pastime. Turn the page and explore everything from fond memories of somersaulting off speedboats and the challenge of learning to swim as an adult to a correspondent's confession about his soft spot for skinny-dipping. Oh, and the one where the writer has absolutely no intention of ever getting wet.

I.
The joy of decks
By Grace Charlton
There's no bigger buzz than the leap from boat to big blue, says our somersaulting scribe.

Time tends to slow down when you're suspended in mid-air. I could spend my life chasing that split second between launching myself off the dry timber deck of a boat and the full-body immersion into the water below, every nerve ending electrified by the drop in temperature. Underwater, the silence envelops you. As you gaze down and decide to take the plunge, diving becomes a joyful and fearless answer to the call of the abyss. There is no better place to swim than off the helm of a see-sawing vessel, straight into the deep end.

Every September, a group of us gather in the Liguria region of Italy to soak up the last of the summer sun. Days drift by as we gorge on the region's famous *trofie al pesto* in San Fruttuoso, ride our bikes along the coast and hike between the colourful fishing villages of Cinque Terre. But the most cherished days are the ones we spend on our friend's speedboat, crammed on top of one another and holding on for dear life as he deftly navigates the waves.

Don't get me wrong, the Mediterranean is perfectly enjoyable from a beach and the Italians have mastered *la dolce far niente* (the sweetness of doing nothing) under yellow-and-white striped parasols. But far from the madding crowd is where you'll find me. Europop anthems will be unashamedly blasting from the speakers as we pick up speed and go rollicking over the waves, with the occasional bone-shaking thud downwards after an ill-timed clip of a crest.

The grey rock formations, bushy landscapes and picturesque hamlets of the Ligurian coast can be better admired from the sea. Our most pressing issue becomes choosing which idyllic spot to drop anchor; we chase down the perfect patch that has taken on the hue of lapis lazuli velvet. The first dip of the day beckons as the heat builds up and we slide into the sea. We might venture onto a rock formation and somersault down. I'm also content to bob around like a duck. Come lunchtime, a feast of focaccia and prosecco is passed around and the day takes a more languorous turn. Cat naps, reading a summer guilty pleasure, alternating between towel and water; these three actions would be on a loop for the rest of my life if I had a choice in the matter.

Admittedly, access to a speedboat provides a certain ease and a flash factor. However, I have managed to capture a similar feeling of freedom by propelling myself off a sailing boat and into the crisp and murky English waters of the Solent. A hired pedalo on Lake Geneva also makes for an effective diving board (just beware of the swans). The means of transportation doesn't affect the ultimate goal: I can defy gravity, for just a little while, before the inescapable submersion.

About the writer: Grace Charlton is a writer and researcher at MONOCLE. Her preferred swimming style can be described as "leisurely" and is often accompanied by a summer spritz.

2.

Lane sailing

By Alexis Self

Our lap-swimming, Speedo-wearing writer on the hypnotic effect of the indoor pool.

There are millions of column inches devoted to the edifying pleasures of a wild dip but no equivalent corpus exists for lane swimming. Lane swimmers like it that way – there's nothing worse than an overcrowded pool. They have a capacity limit: in a standard-sized municipal pool – 25-metres long – it's around four people per section. If everyone respects the space, and one another, this should allow for consistent aquatic movement of, at full pool capacity, 20 bodies. This is a moving sight to behold.

My earliest memory of the effect swimming pools can have on people was as a schoolboy. I attended a Catholic primary school on Brook Green in West London. It was well resourced in the human department but lacked the facilities of its neighbour: St Paul's Girls' School, one of the most august education institutions in Britain, possibly the world. As an act of charity, the administrators of St Paul's allowed the pupils of my school to use their swimming pool once a week. Year groups took it in turns, so that each class would have use of the pool one morning every month. The walk between schools was a short one but the members of our swimming party were no less rambunctious as a result. No doubt many were keen to stamp their bravado on a space that emanated money and privilege. The changing rooms echoed to the sounds of feral laughter but when the 40 or so schoolchildren shuffled through the entrance to the pool, the calming effect was instant. This was the first time I had seen so many people silenced by an empty room. It's not that they were intimidated, they were stilled and could instantly feel themselves in the space.

The only other places that are similarly impactful are religious or expensive. But one's respect for these are bound up in the belief systems and status they represent.

Whereas swimming pools, especially of the municipal variety, exist entirely for our pleasure and leisure, no matter who we are. There's something that will remain forever beguiling about the sensorial effects of a large tiled room filled with water. The way the reflection of the light on the water dances over every surface. The echo that carries a conversation 50 metres away. And, of course, the feeling of cold tile underfoot as you brace yourself for the meeting of two elemental quantities: body and water.

Swimming is the purest form of exercise. It requires no equipment and prohibits the disinhibiting effects of electronic technology. The writer Mark Greif decried gym exercise as an attempt by modern desk-bound humans to mimic the metronomic labour of their industrial and agricultural forebears. Lane swimming is repetitive but its movements serve no commercial purpose – unless your great-grandparents were pearl divers. It is an activity mediated by time but not in the strict capitalistic sense. Most public swimming pools have an analogue clock-face presiding over the scene but only the most serious lane swimmers will use this to time their individual lengths. The majority will enter the pool with the desire to complete a certain number, however long it may take. As they kick off, or dive in, they literally immerse themselves in an activity – a rare pleasure in a world saturated with distraction. In the pool there is only one objective, and it's a worthwhile one: to swim to the other end.

About the writer: Alexis Self is MONOCLE's foreign editor. He is a keen lane swimmer who once competed for the London borough of Hammersmith & Fulham. Self aspires to wear Speedos when he swims but is often spotted in trunks.

3.
Turning the tide
By Francheska Melendez

Learning to swim was a challenge that also taught our writer about her place in the natural world.

Jumping off a seven-metre-high cliff into the sea is not the best idea if you have any doubts about your swimming abilities. When I emerged on the rocky cove, soaking wet, hair matted with seaweed and gasping for air, my then-boyfriend said to me with a frantic smile, "But don't you feel alive?"

One thing became clear to me at that moment: I had to learn to swim properly. I'd spent the previous couple of days bobbing along Mallorca's placid shores, doing a fairly decent doggy paddle while occasionally rolling onto my back to tan my face. I had no reason to doubt that these aquatic skills would prove sufficient in such welcoming waters. But then I decided to dive off a cliff.

"Travelling is a fool's paradise," wrote Ralph Waldo Emerson. The 19th-century US essayist posited that a traveller's pursuit of beauty far from home represents a sort of fleeing from the sad and unrelenting self. According to Emerson, those issues await no matter how far one strays: "My giant goes with me wherever I go." Learning to swim was my giant. It represented a door that had remained firmly shut in my life. If I could open it, the whole ocean awaited. The seeds of my frustration were sown in my native New York City, where children of the Caribbean diaspora like me rarely learn to swim. As a result of limited access to facilities, few parents would consider investing significant time and money to build a skill that didn't seem all that practical in the day-to-day.

As a child, I was lucky enough to spend time on the beaches of the Dominican Republic and Puerto Rico where my parents were born – yet we rarely swam. Seaside life with my relatives revolved around music, storytelling and eating. Raucous laughter and brassy merengue music booming from massive speakers made for a joyful cacophony, drowning out the gently lapping waves as my cousins and I splashed on the shore. I felt at home near the sea but I never grasped how to move weightlessly through it. Even as an adult, my mind boggled that humans could propel themselves through water with coordinated limb movements. That's how I came to think of swimming – not as a way to flow with water but as a series of mechanical strategies to battle against it, overcoming the body's devastating propensity to sink.

When I finally learned to swim, I didn't exactly bust down that philosophical door. Success came in small, hard-won increments. I celebrated every part that clicked into place with deep appreciation. It was a victory when I found I could adjust my breathing according to my physical effort, when I learned to look ahead mid-stroke so I could shift my direction when swimming in open water, when I dove headfirst into a lake even though I had no idea what lurked in that emerald abyss.

It took about eight years but learning to swim has helped me understand my whole body in the context of the wider world. The ocean, the sea, a river or a lake – they are separate bodies from mine with their own ways of moving. Water has its own power and its own peace that behave as two sides of the same coin.

On a recent summer afternoon, I stared out into the Atlantic Ocean from Portugal's southwestern coast. I had swum into a sea cave with my young son. Together, we excitedly searched for fish and crabs before coming to rest on the warm sand. As the salty water dried on our skin, it felt as though I had bid my giant farewell on that shore. I smiled into the ocean breeze, wondering when I might meet another of my giants and bid them farewell too.

About the writer: Francheska Melendez is a Madrid-based writer for MONOCLE and our quarterly sister publication *Konfekt*. Swimming against the tide, in the philosophical sense, has led her to take on all manner of adult-learning scenarios with aplomb, no matter how potentially humiliating.

4.
No place like home
By James Chambers

A swimming pool in the backyard is a fantasy realised for our Asia editor, even if his is a little frigid.

I never dreamed that I would have my own swimming pool. Growing up in South Wales, it was almost unheard of. Daft, even, given the drizzly weather. Backyard pools were something that only existed on television – mainly, it seemed, in California. I spent my childhood going to the local outdoor pool and the beautiful beaches of the Gower. To my memory, the water temperature was always icy cold. I shudder at the thought of taking the plunge on a brisk January day and yet I have always found great comfort in being next to a large body of water, close enough to hear the lapping or crashing waves.

I do some of my best thinking in a (warm) shower and, when away on a reporting trip somewhere in Asia, I like nothing more than the luxury of heading to the hotel pool after nightfall and doing a few leisurely laps of breaststroke. It is while swimming on autopilot – back and forth, back and forth, back and forth – that I go over all of my interviews and think of that all-important opening line of an article. Water is a reliable muse and it just so happens that I'm writing this next to a swimming pool in Bangkok, where I'm now based.

I went through my biggest dry spell for almost a decade while living in London; the water seemed so far away and the swimming options so lacklustre. Spending a few years in an apartment beside the Thames and commuting by riverboat was one, admittedly fortunate, consolation but it was only when I moved to Asia that I plunged back into the water – and the idea of living with a pool took root. It may have taken me another decade and a move from Hong Kong to Bangkok but I have finally made it; kind of. Yes, as a tenant, I can't make any actual claims to ownership of "my" pool in the Thai capital, and I also have to share "my" pool with every other resident of my apartment block (alongside a few thirsty crows). But

it also makes me feel like I'm back in those hotel pools, swimming back and forth, letting my mind wander.

I now have the option to drop everything, pop on a pair of trunks, take the lift down a few floors and dive straight into a swimming pool, in the open air, under the gaze of a golden temple with a huge Thai flag fluttering overhead. That's a luxury I never thought I would have. The one thing that keeps me grounded is that the water is absolutely freezing. My pool has been built in the shade of our building so it hardly sees the sun – much to the delight of my Thai neighbours. One thing I've learned about living in Asia is that hotel swimming pools are busiest after dark, when there's no risk of getting a tan. The thought of heating the water has crossed my mind but in tropical Thailand that would be just as daft as wasting millions on an outdoor pool in South Wales. Which leaves me just where I started, standing on the side of a pool, trying to pluck up the courage to jump in.

About the writer: James Chambers is MONOCLE's Asia editor. His swimming career almost ended as a young boy when a mean instructor shouted at him and he stormed out of the lesson. Chambers has managed to stay afloat on every (non-frozen) continent, despite little more than a 10-metre badge to his name.

5.
Naked attraction
By Robert Bound

Never sneer at the spontaneous skinny-dipper, for there is no finer way to take the plunge.

As this book attests, the urge to submerge is often irresistible. You've likely read that swimming is excellent exercise but practised better as ritual than recreation, more noble as happy habit than as regime, that it's more a sacrament than a sport. It's true that there is something singular and self-absorbed about the swimmer, half-submerged, inching through their scant drop of Earth's vastest, most unknowable element and, out of respect to it, ideally stirring the merest ripple.

And then there's skinny-dipping. Now, skinny-dipping can raise a snort of laughter or at least a suggestive smirk when mentioned in proximity to the more philosophical musings on the nature of water and our historical and habitual relationship with its healing powers and depthless dangers. But, frankly, that's an outrage! To meet fresh water or the bristling brine unencumbered by clinging cotton or bulging nylon is to be born again and to truly understand the subtleties of time and tide – and, particularly, temperature (remember the expectation that management printed on latter-day cereal boxes: "Contents may have settled in transit"?). Brrrr! Skinny-dipping, then, is the *real* real deal.

It's good to bear in mind that skinny-dipping is slightly different to simply bathing sans costume and it's certainly not to be confused with the naturists who just happen to have dropped their drawers and set up their volleyball net by the beach. As we all know, nudists are the last sort of people you'd ever want to see nude, so let's park them well away from the beauty spots that we shall be exploring.

Skinny-dipping is a lot about *frisson*. About time and place and personalities – and all about feeling. You can premeditate the dash-and-dip but it is mostly what that phrase suggests and how it sounds: spontaneous, instinctive, immediate.

It's a guerrilla operation at its best. Time and place is vital to the vibe because it will often be a stolen moment, a refreshing dive into some cool, sane water in a hot, mad place or performed with a naughty glint in the eye and a knowing ignorance of what might happen next. Approach with curiosity, of course, and as much caution as you're content with, please: skinny-dipping is not strong-arming. It's good, clean, dirty fun.

That feeling, the *fuck-it-let's-go*-ness of the spur of the moment could strike at any time. It's like a joke or a kiss – it just happens, sweeps you along with its own momentum when you (might) least expect it. Don't necessarily close your eyes and imagine this but this correspondent has skinny-dipped with friends, lovers, colleagues, members of the art-world elite, two characters who left their guns and ammunition on the beach while they frolicked in the waves and, of course, perfect strangers. The right-place-right-time thing was vital on a trip to tour the vineyards of Portugal's Douro Valley. My old pal handily knew a couple of the surnames above the door of those august port wine lodges in the hills and had cleverly shouldered a waterproof backpack in Porto. So, after devouring plates of cold cuts, sardines and cheese and yet more heavily over-filled glasses of ruby-ripe port, we broke for the only border we could see: the cool, languorous river beyond a small jetty. Our kit flew off so easily in the heat and we were in, splashing and gasping and laughing our heads off in the midsummer flow that had kept a touch more of its high-valley chill than we were expecting. It was cool and glorious, it was tonic and bliss – to spin downriver on the current as we gazed in a happy daze up at the hills and vines that had bestowed on us such giddiness. And then down to the next lodge for a drop more, naturally. The birthday suit makes for quite the commute.

As with any endeavour, personnel are important. Who's in? Well, you'd be surprised. We won't go into the vital statistics of the other bylines swimming through these pages but suffice to say that skinny-dipping is not unknown to this particular media brand. Work can take you to wonderful places and I'll mention Miami because the city is possessed of so many dipping opportunities that you can be like John Cheever's *The Swimmer* and drunkenly make your way home – or to wherever you believe it to be that night – through the low-lit pools of the smart hotels on Collins Avenue. All without wearing so much as a stitch. Grab a towel at the last one though please – hotel lobbies can be sniffy about, well, let's call them tan lines...

A naked swim in nature is a wonderful, life-affirming thing where not a bit of you isn't attuned to the world of water around you. You sense more, you swim better, you're more free, more of a fish or a seal. You're *there*. Orsippus was the first athlete to bust free of his Spartan Speedos (loin cloth) at the Olympics and was seen to have such an advantage that it became de rigueur for other competitors to "run free". That could be you. Oh, but a skinny-dip in a city is a whole different kind of affirmation. It's a thrill, it's a dare, it's the ultimate elemental separation between your becalmed, frog-eyed view of the world and the suits and boots and bustle of the streets. You have reclaimed something by wearing nothing.

Once, in tidy old Zürich, high spirits had been taken and on the way back to the hotel we stopped to gaze at the moonlight shimmering on the rippled mirror of the lake. A handful of us stripped and dipped, we swam to a jetty and lay looking back at the city, seeming strangely distant from our colony of giggles. Back on the shore, a stone's throw from the trams and life – and once the shrieks of delight had become a glow of kinship – one of them turned and said, "I really like your white trunks." Not everyone, then, is sniffy about tan lines. Just remember where you hid your clothes.

About the writer: Robert Bound is a Monocle Radio presenter and senior correspondent and founding member of MONOCLE. He loves swimming (with or without trunks).

6.
For those about to rock
By Sophie Grove
How a distant offshore landmark became a standout achievement on a Spanish summer holiday.

In the early morning, when the tide is high, the rock is barely visible in the water, like a static shark's fin out at sea. But by lunchtime the jagged brown pyramid dominates the view. Here, on the coast of southern Spain, the rock is a fixation. "Have you been to the rock yet?" is an opening gambit for any newcomer unfurling their towel. It is like a buoy for our daily swims – a beacon of achievement before a lunch of grilled sardines in the beachside *chiringuito*.

To swim to the rock is to really contend with the sea. The first stretch in the shelter of the cove feels easy but beyond this – a bit further into the arc of the Bay of Cádiz – the sheer force of the Atlantic makes itself known. Here, the waves start to whip up and there's a sense of a deep expanse of dark blue water below. The only reassuring thing is the rock, our refuge.

Wait for the right moment in the swell and it is possible to heave yourself onto the rock and lie like a lizard on the warm surface, or wave to the people on the sand – assuming that they are impressed. Such a moment is captured in Mary Atkinson's 2010 poem, "Swimming to the Rock", where she observes her brothers capering about; kings of their own little island for a few minutes. "I can't see it but I know their hands are in fists," she wrote. "I can't hear it but I know they are cheering."

A celebration is obligatory for rock swimmers. Back on land there's the sense that you've conquered something and there are rewards. You've never deserved that *cerveza* quite so much. You swam to the rock today.

About the writer: Sophie Grove is the editor of *Konfekt* and executive editor at MONOCLE. She takes every opportunity to swim in lakes, pools and ponds but especially loves the Atlantic surf.

7.
Pool Britannia
By Sophie Monaghan-Coombs
The revival of the UK's public lidos is a testament to the timeless pleasures of these urban oases.

The lido – despite the UK's infamously temperamental weather – is a beloved British cultural institution. In fact, there are more than 100 outdoor pools spread across the island nation. Most are unheated, many are seasonal and they come alive in the warmer months when families jostle for precious poolside space alongside young professionals, fitness enthusiasts and octogenarians. While all of them heave with bodies in the summer, those that operate year-round have some hardy fans who, no matter the weather, will brave biting temperatures in search of a swim.

Dense neighbourhoods and the non-stop nature of modern life can make it hard to find places to slow down – especially as not everyone has access to green space. Yet the lido – a blue rather than grassy patch – offers a different perspective on the city. Open to the skies but simultaneously walled in, the lido provides swimmers with glimpses of the hustle and bustle beyond the pool's boundaries. They are unique in their ability to offer respite from the city when you're at the very heart.

London's lidos each hold their own charm: the Serpentine is carved out of a stretch of the famous lake; Brockwell boasts art deco buildings; Tooting Bec is surrounded by colourful changing huts. But, in addition to those that are well used and loved, a number across the city have been lost. Community campaigns have been crucial in saving some and there are hopes that others might be resurrected: one example is Peckham Lido, which has remained closed since 1987. It was built in response to the pressures of the First World War and Europe's newfound interest in communal exercise. At the time, London County Council leader Herbert Morrison went so far as to christen London a "city of lidos". On top of the health benefits, public baths became significant spaces of relative social freedom. As well as permitting public interaction between the sexes, so too were they stripped of the markers of social status once the swimmers had disrobed.

In the 1970s, the popularity of taking bracing dips in the UK began to drop. Swimmers swapped the country's lidos for warmer waters as cheap flights and package holidays made European sunshine much more accessible. However, a decade later in the 1980s, a renewed interest in modernist architecture helped spearhead an appreciation for these heritage structures.

Nowadays, UK lidos serve all members of the community, whether their pursuits are sporty or social. Over the past century, the lidos that have survived – or those that have been reborn – haven't really changed in their offering or presentation. These iconic outside pools stand as a perennial reminder that sometimes simplicity provides the most peaceful oasis of all.

About the writer: Sophie Monaghan-Coombs is a producer on Monocle Radio. She spent much of her childhood in the unglamorous indoor pools of south-east London and is now much happier lounging beside the water at her local lido.

8.

Merrily down the stream
By Tom Webb

Where better to work through life's problems than on a tipsy river-tubing trip along a river?

As a long-time wild swimmer, I've learned that the first rule is don't drink. As a long-time drinker, I've found that the first rule is, usually, don't swim. How delicious it was to finally marry the two pastimes in the safety of a life raft. If somebody told me the secret to happiness was an inflatable and a can of IPA, I could have saved myself a lot of money. Now, I spend every sunny day that I can bobbing down a wild river, a trashy radio station playing while I clutch a cold one. Floating through the birthplace of William Shakespeare in Stratford-upon-Avon (the very stretch that inspired Bottom's song in *A Midsummer Night's Dream*) is where you'll find me contemplating who performed the greatest cover version of The Rolling Stones's "Sympathy For The Devil".

This focusing of the mind is what first attracted me to river tubing – the act of drifting down a waterway on a rubber inflatable. A good friend once told me that the best way to solve a relationship problem is with a walk in the countryside. River tubing, as I discovered on my first voyage, trumps this.

My new hobby was born in the only nation that could possibly have conceived this earthly delight: the US. In springtime, Hill County in Texas is a day-tripper's paradise. Bluebonnets flower on every corner, barbecues puff smoke in state parks and the air fills with the sound of live music. The real attraction, however, is found on the banks of the Guadalupe River in Kerrville, the capital of Texas Hill Country. Snaking between San Antonio and Austin, the river is the embodiment of slow living. Its gentle bends and sleepy riverside trees make for arguably the world's greatest playground for those seeking life-affirming recreation. Welcome to the world of the lazy river. Straight off the back of a week at the SXSW

Festival in Austin, my sleep-deprived partner and I hit the Guadalupe with nothing but an inflatable tube. Actually, that's not quite true – we opted for the premium experience and paid for a floating cooler packed filled with cans of Hazy Little Thing. What could possibly go wrong?

Slow-living seekers can choose a two, four or six-hour trip. We needed to decompress so it was always going to be the epic option. The ride provided rippled beauty, fresh green leaves and springtime birdsong. My partner and I chatted, like we did as teenagers, in love and with no distractions or responsibilities. We laughed like we did when we had no money or property. We were lovers again rather than partners muddling through the bureaucracy of life. But the more beer that was consumed, the more the untamed Guadalupe navigated us into dangerous waters: as the topic drifted towards the in-laws, things got so spiky that I feared my tube might rupture at any moment.

However, time is a healer and by hour six, when we reached the final bend, we were holding hands, two cells bumping together down Texas's great artery. A yellow school bus waited for us, the driver well briefed on how to handle those who've been drinking all day. As I clambered up the bank, the booze found its way to my legs. I collapsed into the driver's arms and was carted into the vehicle. What a thrill to be on the back row of a bus, dripping wet and giggling like a naughty schoolboy once more.

About the writer: Tom Webb is MONOCLE's deputy head of radio. Webb grew up by the sea and loves swimming every day; moving to London wasn't going to change that, much to the annoyance of rowers on the River Thames.

9.
Deep impact
By Jessica Bridger
Smart city planners are getting wise to the major quality of life benefits that urban bathing brings.

Some of the best times you can have in a city are when you are wearing as little clothing as possible. After all, cities – the best of them at least – are about access, openness, transparency and freedom. Urban swimming requires all four of these qualities and it is a great way to strip down and get to know the places you love a little better. Imagine flying to Zürich for a morning meeting. With a free afternoon in the right season, you can head to the lake, throw down a towel at a *badi*, swim, lie in the sun, enjoy a spritz – and take off again by 18:15.

While you're in this urban oasis, life continues all around: workers toil at desks in nearby office buildings and trams trundle by. Meanwhile, a few people dive into the water in the middle of the day, in the middle of the city – momentarily leaving everything behind. I like urban swimming so much that I moved to one of its global hotspots: Switzerland. Yet a dip in the water is not something that any of us should take for granted – a lot has to be put in place before you can dive into the depths.

Let's start with a basic requirement: the water has to be clean. Many towns once depended on their waterways for transportation and industry, and many still do. Industry, transport and utilities tend to pollute water, which means many of the cities that you can bathe in today – Zürich, Vienna and Boston to name a few – first had an ecological reckoning and treatment measures applied to their watersheds. We can swim now because rivers and lakes became clean, not because they always were.

Next, social convention has to permit people to strip down, show their bodies and be open enough to let the culture thrive. I've seen people in bathing outfits designed for modesty in the Arabian Gulf and *Freikörperkultur* ("free body culture")

fans on the Isar river in Munich. I choose the middle ground, favouring Mara Hoffman's colourful bikinis or the tasteful, textured one-pieces from Paula Beachwear.

Take it off, put it on, swimming in the city is like doing anything else in an urban environment – there's always going to be an audience (you are in public, after all). You can learn a lot about an area from what you see when submerged. Different places have different body cultures. The Swiss, for example, have a surprising penchant for tattoos. It turns out there are more than a few people with full sleeves beneath their bespoke tailoring.

The appeal of city swimming is clear. For the past decade or so, there's been a trend towards planners and designers pushing for more urban bathing. There's recognition that the simple act of floating in the sun, in the city, can make a meaningful contribution to quality of life.

There's ample space for urban swimming to become possible even in places where the culture is not quite open enough or the water not quite as clean as it could be. There's always room for improvement; it just takes a little civic engagement, political will and the ability to dream of something other than the usual configurations of concrete, cars and trees. As you lie beside sparkling water, with city life pulsing around you, it's hard not to feel a deep love for the richness of urban living.

About the writer: When not swimming or skiing, MONOCLE contributing editor Jessica Bridger is an urbanist, journalist and consultant. She travels often and always packs a swimsuit.

10.
The lake show
By Amy van den Berg
Welcome to the dock, a floating summer paradise in Ontario's cottage country.

Summer in Canada is frenzied and feverish, and cottage country – a forested, lake-speckled area in Ontario – is ground zero. As if forgetting that the sun can shine so bright and exposed skin can be so warm, urban Ontarians flock en masse to this rural, cottage-dotted corner in June and let the melancholy of a seven-month-long winter evaporate into the blue sky until September slips into autumn. There are infinite things to do on the many lakes here, and we've mastered them all – from water-skiing and canoeing to dozing on an eclectic and never-ending inventory of inflatable objects (think flamingos, castles and even a trampoline).

My family bought our cottage when I was a teenager. We visited year-round: skating on the frozen water in winter and canoeing around the vibrant russet and yellow-hued lake in the autumn. But the summer is always when it comes alive. At 16:00 on a midsummer's day, the sun is high and the floating dock shines with post-swim puddles, the decking strewn with crumpled towels and open paperbacks. A tray of fresh-cut pineapple and green grapes arrives, cans of Mott's Clamato Caesars (a Canadian twist on a bloody Mary) are opened and, for a while, all feels right in the world.

Over the years, the cottage became a favourite escape for me and my friends: the dock is where I first tasted a grapefruit mimosa, and those same planks have been the launch point for too many moonlit dips to count (sometimes skinny, fuelled in part by the mimosas). Here we've tanned, laughed and drifted lazily in the water.

I now live in London but when I'm in Canada, my family and I spend as many long sunny days at the cottage as we can. Between early walks in the forest and board games at night, we lie in the sun, talking and arguing and napping to the sound of water gently lapping. Somewhere distant, a loon calls.

Our lake is shallow and, while it's no Como, it's quiet and warm. When it gets too hot, it's time to jump back in. The trick is a shallow dive – never feet first or you'll end up two-feet deep in silt. This suspended moment is my favourite place to come back to when the city is loud and the British clouds gather in shades of grey. In my mind, I plunge into the inky depths. When I resurface the first thing I see are the pines that encircle us and I hear laughter from the dock. I look back, and there they are.

About the writer: Amy van den Berg is the deputy editor of MONOCLE's book publishing department. She doesn't condone drinking and swimming, although she accepts that it does happen sometimes.

II.

Club rules

By Chiara Rimella

A step-by-step guide to the Italian 'bagno'. Clue: there's more to it than just sunbathing.

A common misconception about Italians sees them as passionate, sometimes chaotic people who behave instinctively, led by their emotions. Those who believe in such a characterisation have clearly never been to a *bagno* – one of the thousands of beach clubs that line the country's coast – in August.

Life in Italy is, in fact, governed by hundreds of unspoken and often inflexible behavioural rules that range from when it is appropriate to have a cappuccino (only ever in the morning) to how late you can be for a university lecture (that goes for the professor too). Nowhere is this concentration of rules more evident than at the *bagno*. Beach life in Italy isn't about carefree relaxation; it's a seasonal adjustment of everyday lives. In short, people don't leave their "usual" selves behind when they go on holiday: they simply transition into their summer personalities. You may be surrounded by a different cast but you still come with a reputation to uphold.

In a strictly Foucauldian sense, a *bagno* is a power structure. You need only look at the neat arrangement of sunloungers and umbrellas to understand that a hierarchical system is at play. Many of the *postazioni* (stations comprising two beds and an umbrella) have historically been assigned on a seasonal basis – meaning they have belonged to the same family for June, July and August – at a small fortune for years.

Nowadays, working habits have shifted and people no longer have months to spend away from their desks but the way desirable spots at a *bagno* are assigned still depends on assiduity and faithfulness to the establishment (the closer to the sea or to the grid's edges, the better). Crucially, many would never dream of changing which *bagno* they pick – that kind of treason wouldn't go unnoticed. While many Europeans enjoy discovering new countries or beaches each summer, there's an instinct at the core of all Italians that seems to drag them back to the same spot time and again. Even the terminology differs: *fare un viaggio* (going on a journey) is the kind of thing you do off-season. *Andare in vacanza* (going on holiday) is what happens when you relocate to the coast for a while – and it goes without saying that it refers to somewhere within the country's borders.

Of course, traditions are becoming more tenuous than they used to be in the *bagno*'s 1960s heyday. Despite being born in the 19th century as bathing spots for the aristocracy, the concept came into its own when the country was emerging (smiling and covered in sun cream) from the rubble of the Second World War. Back then, beach culture was entirely homegrown because most people couldn't afford to go any further than the closest patch of water to their city apartments, and would load up their Fiat 500s with all the necessary tools for a time in the sun. Today, there are plenty of twenty and thirty-somethings who no longer want to spend their entire summers on the Ligurian litoral – and who pine for Mykonos instead. But the power of childhood memories still has an impressive hold on most minds, which is why the appeal of a proper *vacanza* is hard to turn down. And so the custom continues to be faithfully passed down through generations. But back to the rules – here's a helpful guide to surviving a summer at the *bagno*.

I.

Keep your friends close
Heading to the same spot every year means, by extension, that the people around you will also return every summer. This creates temporary communities with well-defined roles (but also a potential for occasional surprises if fortunes or looks should dramatically change year-on-year). These are, of course, a hotbed of recurring teenage infatuations but also a chance for grown ups to mix, make social comparisons and, occasionally, forge genuine friendships. The right level of involvement – or perhaps ignoring – of your umbrella neighbours is an art that's perfected over the years. Too much conversation and you'll come off as nosey; not enough and you'll be branded as conceited. In the stillness of the August heat, a dance of manners is constantly underway.

2.

Come prepared

It is perfectly acceptable – if not encouraged – to bring your own packed lunch to the beach. It denotes preparedness and unwillingness to be swindled by the system, which is an Italian's utmost source of pride. (Everybody knows the beach restaurant's salads will be overpriced and unlikely to be as good as anything homemade, although the rule does come undone in the presence of a good *fritto misto*.) In fact, the more elaborate, the better: cold pasta is ideal, accompanied by fresh fruit. Meagre sandwiches are unlikely to get you anywhere. Slices of coconut may be purchased from the men shouting *"cocco bello"* and selling bucketfuls while walking up and down the beach – but only a couple of times per week, as a gesture of goodwill for the local economy. The shaded terrace of the restaurant can be used in the hottest hours of the afternoon for a coffee, maybe an ice-cream, or just to get a break from the sand. Most people will be encouraged to consume their beverage and leave space for other customers but no-one should even think about suggesting the group of over-eighties engaged in a long game of cards should be moved along. They've probably been coming here since before you were born.

3.

Dress for the occasion

Until you've taken your position under the umbrella, it is preferable to wear an outfit that covers chest and bum. For the women, that's often a so-called *copricostume* ("swimsuit-coverer") – a frilly beach dress that only sees the light of day in the months of July and August, emerging from the dark recesses of a wardrobe. Visits to the beach-side restaurant don't necessarily require full redressing but some degree of effort is recommended – even donning one extra item of clothing will be appreciated.

4.

The daily programme

As for activities, these can involve occasional games of paddle tennis by the *bagnasciuga* (the water's edge) or a very special spin on a branded pedalo. However, days should mainly consist of lying in the sun, reading or filling in crosswords. Hyperactivity will not be tolerated – not within the forest of sun umbrellas, at least. And finally, songs. It is likely the *bagno* will be playing one of the nation's radio stations, blaring out the season's hits whether you like it or not. It is pointless to resist this in search of a moment of silence. Embrace a chance to witness the annals of music history being written and be thankful that your neighbour isn't playing their favourite track, the tinny tune blaring out of the phone speakers. After all, these summertime songs are called *tormentoni* ("tormenters") for a reason. Whoever said beach life was just about enjoyment, anyway?

About the writer: Growing up in Italy, MONOCLE's executive editor Chiara Rimella spent most of her summers jumping into Sardinia's waters. Her reporting has spanned most disciplines but her favourite assignments are those that allow for a quick dip – be that on a Californian beach or in a geothermal pool in Reykjavík.

12.

Persons of interest

By Natalie Theodosi

Assigning stories to fellow beach-goers is a healthy holiday pursuit. So let your imagination run free.

I've been a fan of people-watching for as long as I can remember. Growing up, there was nothing I loved more than quietly observing adults' outfits and daydreaming about how I would dress as a grown-up. Now, I continue to indulge in people-watching during my daily commute, observing fellow train passengers' looks, the bags they are carrying and the books they are reading. What kind of life might be led, for example, by the elegant woman sporting a pixie haircut and reading Susan Sontag on the London Underground?

But people-watching at its finest takes place at the beach, under clear sunny skies. Perhaps it's because the high temperatures and the decadence of beach clubs encourages everyone to relax and express themselves more freely through fashion, be it long kaftans in mood-boosting hues; swimming trunks in the same bright orange as an Aperol spritz; oversized sunglasses and teeny bikinis. A beach holiday also offers the luxury of time. Rather than a passing glance on the train or street, I can spend hours on a sunlounger looking at fellow beach-goers from underneath the dark lenses of my round-framed Celine sunglasses and letting my imagination run loose about who they might be or what kind of holiday they're on.

During a recent trip to the Athens Riviera (*see page 32*), where days are usually spent between the sandy shores of the popular Astir Beach and its nearby club, I was intrigued by the woman lounging under the umbrella next to mine and the way she was able to translate the best of Parisian dress codes for the beach. She wore a woven, navy-and-white-striped dress, elegant leather slippers by Hermès and an oversized raffia bag – probably sourced at a flea market to ensure its originality. I built a mental picture of her as a high-level executive from Paris, probably working for one of the city's heritage fashion houses. She would be living in an elegant Left Bank apartment, smoking cigarettes on her Haussmannian balcony, frequenting cafés and with a closet full of little black dresses, suits and Chanel 2.55 handbags.

A few sunloungers down was a very different type of woman – larger than life in her wide-brimmed hat, enormous sunglasses and bright orange and pink Pucci kaftan. She commanded attention with her colourful clothing, animated conversation and the way she simply embodied joie de vivre. I was convinced she was the owner of the yacht moored nearby and would soon be picked up and returned to her boat, where she'd have a glass of white wine on the deck, watch the sun set and get ready for dinner. The following day she would continue her Mediterranean adventure to nearby Hydra (*see page 66*), followed by Syros in the Cyclades and finally Mykonos, where she would spend her days sipping champagne, eating seafood pasta at the best beach clubs and dancing Greek *sirtaki* with locals.

Observing this intriguing stranger offered an opportunity for escapism in its most indulgent form. For a few moments I immersed myself in this fantasy of a life where the sun is always shining, lounge music is always playing and the day revolves around dips in crystal clear waters, socialising on plush sunbeds and enquiring about the catch of the day. It's the kind of treat that summer holidays call for, a rare occasion to flex our imaginative muscles and let our minds travel.

About the writer: Natalie Theodosi is MONOCLE'S fashion editor. When she's not travelling between Europe's design capitals and reporting on the luxury industry, she returns to her home of Cyprus and makes the most of the sun, seafood and Mediterranean waters.

13.
Where the wild swims are
By Naomi Xu Elegant
Just beyond Hong Kong's dense cityscape are many wild bathing spots – if you know where to look.

Hong Kong is one of the world's most densely populated regions, its very name conjuring images of skyscrapers and crowded streets. Almost half of its land mass, however, consists of rocky islands, pristine beaches, tropical forests and verdant hills. Hidden in these scenic nooks are beautiful wild swimming spots, unparalleled in their combination of accessibility and isolation. The city's public transport network can take you to the forested peninsulas of Sai Kung and Plover Cove, or to Lantau Island and its sandy bays.

There are many "official" places to swim in Hong Kong, be they hotel pools with cityscape views or packed beaches with lifeguards and shark nets. But straying off course is much more fun. With a bit of persistence, a world of secret beaches and secluded lagoons will open up. Searching for the perfect spot becomes something of a game – scouring maps for dark patches that look like water sources, or razor-thin lines in thick tree coverage that lead the way to otherwise inaccessible beaches. Some of these sites are harder to reach than others: I once mistook a wild boar trail for a hiker's path and found myself teetering on a cliff's edge. As I clutched at flimsy branches and felt small rocks start to roll beneath my feet, I wondered what had possessed me to pursue this pastime. After correcting my course and emerging through a curtain of trees to find a beautiful empty beach, it was easy to remember why. I waded into the ocean and paddled around. I closed my eyes and let the sun warm my face. The sound of cicadas was the only noise I could hear.

About the writer: Naomi Xu Elegant is a Singapore-based writer for MONOCLE. She grew up in the tropics and was once stung by a jellyfish off the coast of Langkawi, which she still finds preferable to cold water swimming.

14.
Lounging at large
By Brenda Tuohy
There are some who would rather be 'beside' the seaside than up to their necks in the ocean.

I've never been much of a swimmer – and I truly hate the ocean. It's nice to lounge next to but I simply can't bear the idea of the soles of my feet touching anything other than sand or the smooth tiles of a swimming pool.

You lose all control when you enter the sea: if the waves swell and crash over your head and knock you over, you have no choice but to gulp down a couple of gallons of seawater as you try to regain composure. You'll eventually emerge with your hair soaked, your make-up running and your throat wretched with salt. Because of this, I choose my water wisely. I often holiday in Dubai surrounded by the Arabian Sea but I swim mainly in pools (chilled or heated depending on the time of year). Although the sea is in plain sight, I ignore it unless it's high summer and as inviting as a warm bath.

I also choose my social group wisely – they know how to dress for the beach. My girlfriends are on my wavelength: Cartier bracelets for Katrina, Van Cleef & Arpels for Veruskha and a Tiffany T for Tatiana. And me, Brenda, swathed in oodles of Boodles diamonds (and sparkling in the sun). If you need me, I'll be on my sunlounger under a large striped umbrella, book open, sipping coconut water and glancing at the glamour-pusses around me. Whether the dress code is burkini or bikini, the make-up is always carefully applied, and hair is wrapped in silk scarves by Hermès or Dior. This is my swimming paradise.

About the writer: A lover of holidays and lazing around in general, Brenda Tuohy has lived in London for more than 30 years and is currently MONOCLE's client director. She is mortally afraid of anything that lurks in the water and of getting her hair wet.

15.

The Japanese Crawl

By Fiona Wilson

From Samurai strokes to pool rules, swimming in Japan is – like much else – a very different entity.

An archipelago nation made up of thousands of islands, Japan is steeped in watery pursuits. Japan's visual and literary history is populated with tales of fisherfolk who depended on the ocean for their livelihood. The famed Ama (literally "sea women"), who pop up in Japan's oldest poetry compilation the *Man'yoshu*, are fewer in number now but still dive into the waters of Mie Prefecture for pearls and seafood, equipped with little more than well-trained lungs and a scuba mask.

For the open swimmer, Japan has it all: oceans, rivers, lakes and mountain streams. Leisure swimmers will want to steer clear of the north's chilly sea, which are populated by giant crabs, hefty tuna and the occasional floating iceberg, but head south to the subtropical seas of Okinawa and there are clear waters, coral reefs and turtles for company. In between, there are hundreds of swimming beaches dotted along the coast which "open" for the summer season, a small window in July and August sandwiched between the misty drizzle of the rainy season and autumnal typhoons.

For most Japanese, though, swimming takes place in a pool. Many serve an athletic purpose and elementary schools in Japan usually have an outdoor space to drill children in the basics. Foreign visitors are sometimes flummoxed by the rigid rules in Japan but they are simple enough: swimming caps, no shoes in the changing room, no visible tattoos or jewellery and you must shower before entering. More surprising to some are the 10 minutes every hour when swimmers get out to sit on the poolside while the lifeguards switch positions and check the water.

Nihon Eiho, Japanese classical swimming, is a more niche pastime. It developed when Japan's endless civil wars drew to a close at the end of the 16th century and the aquatic skills used by Samurai in battle were systematised as a martial art,

known as *suijutsu* (water skills). *Nihon Eiho* practitioners come together for an annual tournament that looks nothing like a conventional swimming competition. It turns out that modern strokes, although speedy, wouldn't have been much use to a Samurai warrior who had to stay afloat in full armour, fight with swords in rivers, or sidestroke for hours with the ebb and flow of the tide. Instead of a high-speed front crawl, classical swimmers compete to show off their prowess at moves such as the "Flying Mullet" or "Crane Dance", and tread water while weighed down. It seems that in swimming, as in so much else, Japan is happy to carve its own path.

About the writer: Fiona Wilson lives in Tokyo and is MONOCLE'S senior Asia editor. She has swum all over Japan, from waterfalls in Kagoshima to surf beaches in Kanagawa. She feels at home with the rules of a Japanese pool and has no problem wearing the requisite swimming hat.

16.
The one-mile club
By Alex Milnes

How swimming can heal even the harshest heartbreaks – and lead to a new way of life.

My love affair with swimming began at the close of another. While forlorn and in need of something to focus on after my girlfriend dumped me, a friend suggested that I start swimming and set myself a goal – such as signing up to the Swim Serpentine one-mile challenge. The annual event sees swimmers complete a full lap of the Serpentine Lake in London's Hyde Park – the same course that was used in the open-water races during the city's 2012 Summer Olympics. I'd never been one for exercise and, apart from the odd dip in the sea, I hadn't swum properly since school. The thought of swimming one mile non-stop, with only six months to hone my skills, was terrifying. Despite this, I signed up to the event and my local pool.

My confidence was low and my strokes weak but from the moment I slipped into the water I felt different. My first concern was making it to the other side of the pool but, as time went on, I learned to front-crawl and I started swimming every morning before work. Soon, I graduated from the slow lane to the medium, and then the fast. I set myself challenges: how quickly could I swim one lap? How many lengths could I do in 30 minutes? My mood was changing and the sadness I once felt was replaced by a new energy. My next challenge was to train outside, so I visited Tooting Bec Lido. At around 90 metres, it is the largest freshwater swimming pool in the UK. Initially daunting, I was soon doing a couple of mornings there too. Swim Serpentine came around and any fears I'd had were gone. Adrenaline and my new-found confidence carried me – I finished quicker than I thought I would.

After the race, I continued swimming as much as I could. I joined different pools as I moved around London, from Brockwell Lido to Hampstead Ponds. In what seems like fate, I've now returned to the Serpentine. Swimming – which is a passion that I share with my now wife – has become more than a hobby. It helps me de-stress, it wakes me up and calms me down. Despite constantly moving, it's the only time of the day that everything else stops. I don't talk, there's no music, podcasts or screens. I'm alone with my thoughts. As Bonnie Tsui writes in *Why We Swim*: "Swimming can enable survival in ways beyond the physical".

About the writer: MONOCLE's photography editor Alex Milnes has swum in beautiful pools and oceans around the world but he enjoys plunging into Hyde Park's Serpentine Lido the most.

6.
Directory

The water's wide and the world is vast – and there are plenty more dips in the sea. In this book, we've presented the pools, beach clubs and hidden oases that we've been lucky enough to visit but there's a world of others to explore. So, we spoke to our editors, friends and writers for their closely-guarded secrets. Here's a list of more than 70 swimming spots to dive into next – we'll see you there.

Bermagui Blue Pool
Australia
A spectacular sea pool between a cliff wall and a rocky ledge in Bermagui that overlooks the Pacific Ocean. Head here for pristine waters teeming with marine life.
Bermagui, New South Wales

Bronte Baths
Australia
One of the country's oldest ocean pools. Its basin is carved dramatically into the area's sandstone headland.
Bronte Road, Sydney

Centenary Pool
Australia
Completed in 1959, this Brisbane complex is a modernist marvel. The site includes three pools, one Olympic-sized, and an elevated kiosk at its centre.
400 Gregory Terrace, Brisbane

Fitzroy Pool
Australia
This outdoor pool in Melbourne was saved from closure in 1994 by the local community. Today it's a neighbourhood hub where swimmers rack up laps and sunbathers doze on concrete steps.
160 Alexandra Parade, Melbourne

Waldbad Lech
Austria
Surrounded by towering trees and mountain peaks, Lech's *waldbad* (forest bath) was renovated in 2022 and comprises four pools; two for adults and two for children.
lechzuers.com

Boekenberg Swimming Pond
Belgium
Boekenbergpark's open-air site in Antwerp is completely natural (it's purified by plant life on the pond bed) and is open from May to September.
Van Baurscheitlaan 88, Antwerp

Flow
Belgium
Brussels' modular canal-side swimming structure is free to visit and open from July to September. It has a compact pool, tiered sun decks and a bar, which livens up come sunset.
flow.brussels

Costa Brava Clube
Brazil
The Costa Brava members' club is set on a rocky promontory overlooking Rio de Janeiro's Joatinga Beach. It has two pools; one on the clifftop and the other, a sea bath, at the water's edge.
costabravaclube.com.br

Hotel das Cataratas
Brazil
A luxury hacienda-style retreat in the heart of the Iguaçu National Park. The swimming pool is surrounded by orchids and lush gardens.
belmond.com

Borden Park Natural Swimming Pool
Canada
Located in Edmonton, this is the first chemical-free outdoor pool in Canada. The water is filtered naturally using plants, layers of gravel and sand.
7615 Borden Park Road NW, Edmonton

Tierra Atacama Hotel & Spa
Chile
This elegant hotel is located in Chile's northern desert. The pool is set within landscaped gardens with panoramic views of the stark, sandy landscape.
tierrahotels.com

ŠC Bazeni Poljud
Croatia
This sports centre in Split boasts an outdoor pool with a set of gleaming, mid-century diving platforms.
jusos.hr

Sun Gardens
Croatia
A 20-minute drive from Dubrovnik, this seaside resort's circular pool overlooks the Elaphiti Islands and the glistening Adriatic.
dubrovniksungardens.com

Odense Havnebad
Denmark
The open-air pool in Odense Harbour has a distinctly seaside theme – it was designed to look like the deck of a ship, complete with nautical changing huts.
Gamle Havnekaj 3, Odense

Vestre Søbad
Denmark
A pair of round wooden bathing bridges form two natural swimming ponds in Lake Almindsø, near Silkeborg. The larger one is for adults and the smaller one is for children.
Søndre Ringvej 1, Silkeborg

Centre Nautique Tony Bertrand
France
Designed by local architect Alexandre Audouze-Tabourin, this complex was built along the banks of the Rhône River for Lyon's failed bid for the 1968 Summer Olympics.
8 Quai Claude Bernard, Lyon

Cercle des Nageurs de Marseille
France
An old-school members' club frequented by the Marseille elite. It was founded in 1921 and offers an exclusive pool on the cliff face.
cnmarseille.com

Molitor
France
These iconic art deco pools reopened as part of this Paris hotel in 2014 following years of disrepair. Today guests can swim where Louis Réard unveiled the first bikini and the topless sunbathing revolution was born.
molitorparis.com

La Colombe d'Or
France
A small family-run hotel in the medieval hilltop village of Saint-Paul-de-Vence. It is known for its private art collection: the emerald pool is decorated with an extraordinary Alexander Calder mobile.
la-colombe-dor.com

Monte-Carlo Beach
France
This hotel in Roquebrune-Cap-Martin is much-loved by France's well-heeled. It has a private beach club and pool with terracotta-toned diving boards.
montecarlosbm.com

Badeschiff
Germany
A public swimming pool in Berlin that floats on the River Spree and offers swimmers a unique view of the city.
arena.berlin

Four Seasons Astir Palace
Greece
Astir Palace opened on the Athens Riviera in 1958 and quickly became a high-flyers' hangout. It's just as popular today and offers three private coves and two swimming pools, complete with cabanas and cocktails.
fourseasons.com

Semuc Champey Natural Monument
Guatemala
In the heart of the Guatemala's jungle is Semuc Champey, a picturesque network of tiered natural limestone pools and waterfalls that are primed for a dip.
San Agustín Lanquín, Guatemala

Laugardalslaug
Iceland
This Reykjavík pool complex is the place to experience Iceland's swimming culture.
Sundlaugavegur 105, Reykjavik

Cola Beach Lagoon
India
This freshwater lake in Goa has an inviting emerald hue and is shaded by arching palms. The lagoon also leads onto Cola Beach, a wide stretch with milk-white sand.
Cola Beach Road, Goa

Kahani Paradise
India
Kahani Paradise is set high in the hills of Karnataka, overlooking the surrounding jungle and Arabian Sea. As its name suggests, the oval-shaped pool is an oasis.
kahaniparadise.com

Potato Head Beach Club
Indonesia
The pool at this cool beachfront hotel on Bali is a relaxing affair. For a more lively dip, head to the group's beach club next door.
seminyak.potatohead.co

Hotel Il Pellicano
Italy
A masterclass in understated luxury, this Tuscan hotel boasts a seawater pool with views of the Tyrrhenian Sea, as well as a private beach club.
hotelilpellicano.com

Piscina Zinzulusa Castro
Italy
This circular saltwater swimming basin in Castro overlooks the Adriatic Sea and is named after a craggy cave nearby.
Via Grotta Del Conte 7, Castro

Halekulani Okinawa
Japan
Not to be confused with the Hawaii outpost of the same name, this resort in Okinawa has five pools (one with the group's signature orchid motif) and a white-sand beach.
okinawa.halekulani.com

Naboisho Camp
Kenya
Guests of this remote lodge in Naboisho Conservancy can watch wildlife pass by while bathing in an infinity-style stone pool.
asiliaafrica.com

Eddésands
Lebanon
This glamorous spot in the seaport of Byblos includes a serviced beach (complete with double-bed loungers) and five pools.
eddesands.com

Saint-George Yacht Club & Marina
Lebanon
Dating from 1934, this Beirut seafront club is nothing short of legendary – it remained open during the civil war and survived a car bomb in 2005. It has two pools and a cocktail bar.
stgeorges-yachtclub.com

Baja Club
Mexico
The secluded courtyard and glistening lap pool at this La Paz hotel is as serene as it gets.
bajaclubhotel.com

Carpa Olivera
Mexico
An ocean pool in Mazatlán that was built in 1915 and features a curving concrete slide.
P Claussen, Mazatlán

Beldi Country Club
Morocco
This Marrakech hotel has a long blue-tiled pool, thatched cabanas and views of the Atlas Mountains.
beldicountryclub.com

Fairmont Tazi Palace
Morocco
The former residence of the king's adviser, Tazi Palace hotel is a grand affair. The pool is no exception with sweeping views of Tangier.
fairmont.com

Royal Mansour Marrakech
Morocco
A stone's throw from Marrakech's medina, the pool of this regal hotel is enveloped in lush gardens and shaded by date palms.
royalmansour.com

Le Mirage Resort & Spa
Namibia
This hotel in the middle of Namib Desert was designed to appear as an ancient fortress – the ornate pool is the jewel at its centre.
mirage-lodge.com

Lake Rotoiti
New Zealand
Within the Nelson Lakes National Park, this mountain lake is fed by the Travers River and is a wild spot to take a dip. Keep an eye out for the resident (and friendly) longfin eels.
Nelson Lakes National Park, Tasman Region

St Clair Hot Salt Water Pool
New Zealand
A six-lane heated pool on a rocky Dunedin promontory. It offers swimmers stunning views of St Clair beach.
Esplanade, St Clair, Dunedin

Leça da Palmeira Pools
Portugal
This complex, designed by Portuguese architect Álvaro Siza in 1966, comprises two tidal pools, which have been built into the rugged Matosinhos coastline.
Avenida da Liberdade, Leça da Palmeira

Porto Moniz Natural Swimming Pools
Portugal
On the northwestern tip of Madeira are the Porto Moniz Natural Swimming Pools, a network of rocky lava basins that fill with seawater at high tide.
portomoniz.pt

Ada Ciganlija
Serbia
Known as Belgrade's seaside, this river island has been transformed into an urban peninsula complete with a freshwater lake. In the summer, the spot comes alive with bustling beach bars and restaurants.
Ada Ciganlija, Belgrade

Kolezija
Slovenia
Built in 1878, Kolezija is the oldest city bath in Ljubljana. The historical complex was renovated in 2015 and has a modern, Olympic-sized pool.
Gunduliceva Ulica 7, Ljubljana

Miller's Point Tidal Pool
South Africa
A large, circular ocean bath located at the edge of Cape Town on the wild and rocky coast of the Cape Peninsula.
Main Road, Cape Town

Sea Point Pavilion
South Africa
This seaside site in Cape Town has four swimming pools as well as diving platforms for swimmers of all ages.
Beach Road, Sea Point, Cape Town

The Oyster Box
South Africa
A beachfront hotel near Durban known for its striped sunloungers, where guests enjoy views of the pool, the Indian Ocean and the red-and-white lighthouse.
oysterboxhotel.com

Cap Rocat
Spain
In a converted 19th-century fortress in Mallorca's Bay of Palma is the secluded Cap Rocat hotel. It has a dazzling infinity pool plus a handful of suites with private baths cut out of the rockface.
caprocat.com

Parque Marítimo
Spain
Pool complex-cum-sculpture park on Tenerife was designed by local artist César Manrique. It has three salt-water pools, an artificial waterfall and jacuzzi – all dotted with volcanic rocks, palm trees and Manrique's sculptures.
parquemaritimosantacruz.es

Six Senses Ibiza
Spain
This sleek hotel from the Six Senses group has a wide infinity pool that curves along the Cala Xarraca shoreline.
sixsenses.com

The Madrid Edition
Spain
This city-centre hotel has an expansive rooftop pool and terrace bar where smart day beds, parasols and rustling greenery could trick you into thinking you're on the Med.
editionhotels.com

Amangalla
Sri Lanka
From the Aman hospitality group, this hotel is located within the 17th-century Unesco-listed Galle Fort. The green-tiled pool is an urban oasis surrounded by lush gardens.
aman.com

Badi Utoquai
Switzerland
One of Zürich's oldest swimming clubs, this lake-side spot was built in 1890. One side is reserved for women, the other for men and there's a mixed pool in the middle.
Utoquai 50, Zürich

Thanyapura Sports & Health Resort
Thailand
The place to visit for serious swimming, Thanyapura is one of Thailand's largest sports centres and features two eight-lane pools among Phuket's tropical scenery.
thanyapura.com

The Peninsula Bangkok
Thailand
This grand hotel's three-tier swimming pool stretches out towards the Chao Phraya River and is lined with spacious cabanas.
peninsula.com

The Racquet Club
Thailand
A club in Bangkok that offers sports facilities as well as three swimming pools and a jacuzzi. You can get certified for scuba diving here, ready for the country's reefs.
rqclub.com

Four Seasons Istanbul at the Bosphorus
Turkey
In a grand 19th-century Ottoman palace on the banks of the Bosphorus, this hotel's outdoor pool is big enough for a proper swim.
fourseasons.com

Maçakizi
Turkey
Drawing a jet-set crowd since it opened in the 1970s, this Bodrum hotel has a private pool but its beach club is the main draw. Bag a lounger on the sun deck for stunning views of the Aegean Sea.
macakizi.com

Jumeirah Al Naseem
UAE
At the centre of this sprawling Dubai hotel is the pool, flanked by palms, daybeds and gardens designed by US landscape architect Bill Bensley. It also boasts views of the iconic Burj Al Arab.
jumeirah.com

Cleveland Pools
UK
On the banks of the River Avon in Bath, this Georgian lido is one of Britain's oldest.
clevelandpools.org.uk

Hampstead Heath Ponds
UK
One of the most visited outdoor swimming spots in London, Hampstead's ponds are comprised of three baths: one for women, one for men and one mixed.
hampsteadheath.net

Jubilee Pool
UK
This art deco lido in Cornwall is Grade-II listed and a local favourite. It's also the largest seawater pool in the UK.
jubileepool.co.uk

Serpentine Lido
UK
An iconic unheated and unchlorinated lido in London's Hyde Park, which was created as an ornamental lake in 1730.
Hyde Park, London

Fasano Las Piedras
Uruguay
The swimming pool at this elegant hotel in Uruguay's countryside near Maldonado has been carved out of the rockface.
laspiedrasfasano.com

Amangiri
USA
Another hotel by the Aman group, Amangiri's unique pool has been designed around a large rock in the middle of the Colorado Plateau in Utah.
aman.com

Annenberg Community Beach House
USA
This public pool sits on the edge of LA's Santa Monica beach in a tiled courtyard that once entertained Hollywood's elite.
annenbergbeachhouse.com

Barton Springs Pool
USA
Zilker Metropolitan Park in Austin is home to this long outdoor bath, which is fed by natural underground springs. The water remains a comfortable 20C all year round.
2201 William Barton Drive, Austin

Catalina Beach Club
USA
This family-run beach club on Long Island's Atlantic Beach has been welcoming members every summer since it opened in 1944. As well as its beach location, it has a swimming pool and colourful painted changing rooms.
catalinabeachclub.com

Surfjack Hotel & Swim Club
USA
In a modernist building near Hawaii's Waikiki Beach, the Surfjack Hotel is much-loved by those in the know. The bottom of the oval-shaped pool is emblazoned with a tongue-in-cheek "wish you were here" slogan.
surfjack.com

Descanso Beach Club
USA
An hour by ferry from LA, Santa Catalina Island is home to this beachside restaurant and bar, the perfect place to enjoy a cocktail with a view of the Descanso Canyon.
1 St Catherine Way, Avalon

The Raleigh
USA
On the Miami beachfront, this art deco hotel has been a cult favourite since the 1940s. Its curved pool was dubbed the most beautiful in the US by *Life* magazine in 1947.
theraleigh.com

SWIM & SUN: A MONOCLE GUIDE

Hot beach clubs | Perfect pools | Lake havens
PLUS: a big splash of sunny après-swim living

Index

Acknowledgements

Monocle

Editorial Director & Chairman
Tyler Brûlé

Editor in Chief
Andrew Tuck

Editor
Molly Price

Deputy Editor
Amy van den Berg

Creative Director
Richard Spencer Powell

Junior Designer
Oli Kellar

Photography Director
Matthew Beaman

Photography Editor
Alex Milnes

Deputy Photography Editor
Amara Eno

Production Director
Jacqueline Deacon

Production Manager
Sarah Kramer

Special thanks
Josh Fehnert
Nick Mee
Joe Pickard
Steve Pill
Amy Richardson
Sonia Zhuravlyova

Researchers
Alexandra Aldea
Mashal Butt
Conor McCann
Lucrezia Motta

Writers

Carolina Abbott Galvão
Liam Aldous
Désirée Bandli
Robert Bound
Jessica Bridger
Tyler Brûlé
James Chambers
Grace Charlton
Guy De Launey
Lucinda Elliott
Sophie Grove
Claudia Jacob
Christopher Lord
Callum McDermott
Francheska Melendez
Alex Milnes
Sophie Monaghan-Coombs
Molly Price
Carlota Rebelo
Chiara Rimella
Laura Rysman
Alexis Self
Ed Stocker
Natalie Theodosi
Andrew Tuck
Brenda Tuohy
Hester Underhill
Amy van den Berg
Tom Webb
Fiona Wilson
Naomi Xu Elegant

Photographers

Marco Arguello
Nicolas Axelrod
Yves Bachmann
Kristin Bethge
Thomas Block Humery
Felix Brüggemann
Rodrigo Cardoso
Silvia Conde
Terence Chin
Alex Crétey Systermans
Bea De Giacomo
Stephanie Füessenich
Stefan Fürtbauer
Victor Garrido
Daniel Gebhart de Koekkoek
Derek Henderson
Mariano Herrera
Andreas Jakwerth
Juho Kuva
Jason Larkin
Salva Lopez
Lit Ma
Benjamin McMahon
Luca Meneghel
James Mollison
Felix Odell
Jonas Opperskalski
Anthony Perez
Maciek Pozoga
Ben Roberts
Matthew Scott
Matilde Viegas
Joe Wigdahl
Dan Wilton
Samuel Zeller
Marvin Zilm

About Monocle

Join our club

In 2007, MONOCLE was launched as a monthly magazine briefing on global affairs, business, design and more. Today we have a thriving print business, a radio station, shops, cafés, books, films and events. At our core is the simple belief that there will always be a place for a brand that is committed to telling fresh stories, delivering good journalism and being on the ground around the world. We're Zürich and London-based and have bureaux in Hong Kong, Tokyo and Los Angeles. Subscribe at *monocle.com*

Monocle magazine

MONOCLE magazine is published 10 times a year, including two double issues (July/August and December/January). We also have annual special, THE FORECAST, and two editions of THE ENTREPRENEURS. Look out for our seasonal weekly newspapers too.

Monocle Radio

Our round-the-clock online radio station delivers global news and shows covering foreign affairs, urbanism, business, culture, food and drink, design and print media. You can listen live or download shows from monocle.com/radio – or wherever you get your podcasts.

Books

Since 2013, MONOCLE has been publishing books such as this one, covering a range of topics from home design and how to live a gentler life, to our country-focused guides. All our books are available on our website, through our distributor Thames & Hudson or at all good bookshops.

Monocle Minute

MONOCLE's smartly appointed newsletters come from our team of editors and bureaux chiefs around the world. From the daily *Monocle Minute* to the *Monocle Weekend Editions* and our weekly *On Design* special, sign up to get the latest in lifestyle, affairs and design, straight to your inbox.